Hello... Anyone Home?

A Guide on How our Deceased Loved Ones

Try to Contact Us through the Use of Signs

Joseph M. Higgins

Hello...Anyone Home?

ISBN 978-0-9825716-0-6
ISBN 0-9825716-0-7

Printed in USA

Dedication

I would like to thank my guides, teachers and loved ones for helping me in my development and for protecting me with the white light of love.

I thank them all for the guidance and insight they have shared with all of us in order to relieve the suffering and grief that we all will experience some time in our lives.

Be kind and love one another.

Peace,
Joe Higgins

Acknowledgments

J want to thank my friend Chuck Bergman for his help working with me in order for my mediumistic abilities to take shape and blossom. You were there in the beginning and we had a lot of fun learning our new skills together.

To my deceased aunt Eileen for inspiring me to write this book by sending me not one but two signs within a week and relieving me of any doubt forever.

To my sister Maureen, for telling me of the signs she has received from family and friends. You know how to understand and truly accept them.

I wish to especially thank Nina, who not only has shown me tremendous support but has opened my heart and filled me with incredible love which I hope I can return.

Table of Contents

❦

Part Three
How Do I Do It?

Contact Section

Introduction

❦

In writing this book, I've used my experiences as a medium to try to enlighten the reader regarding some of the similar concepts of communicating with their departed loved ones.

At times, throughout the book, I have channeled information from my guides on the other side; and, I have tried to leave their communication as close as possible to what they have given to me. However, some slight editing was done in order for the concepts and ideas to flow more easily. I thought it would be very interesting for the readers to be able to have a first-hand opportunity to read guidance and insight from the loving guides who interact with me.

I have also taken the time to comment on some of the stories that are included in the book, as I think they show very good examples of some of the ways that our loved ones use to contact us. These methods that are listed in the stories are just a few of the many ways with which our loved ones try to contact us.

By using my experience as a medium along with the insights and information from my guides as well as some of the examples from the stories provided by friends and family, it is my belief that it is possible to connect with our past loved ones. We can interact with our loved ones as well as gain guidance and insight from loving guides who work with all of us each and every day.

One of the main things I have learned from my experiences is to open up and ask for assistance through prayer. From your heart, ask for assistance in dealing with all the obstacles in your life. Don't expect a magic wand to suddenly make all your problems go away, for this is not how life is supposed to work. Life can be difficult and unforgiving at times, while' at others times' it can be full of joy, love and understanding. I believe that the trick is to try to combine these two reactions and to understand that the most important thing in life is treating others fairly and with respect. That especially includes you. For if you cannot love and respect yourself it is a difficult task to be able to show that to others.

Your loved ones, who have passed to the other side, understand this; and, that is why they wish to contact you to let you know that their existence continues even though their physical body has deteriorated. Their essence has continued on and, with just a small contact, they can let you in on the big picture: that life is not as controlled and limited as they once saw it while they were living on the physical plane.

They realize that a lot of the little things that used to bother them were insignificant and that the meaning of life can be summed up with one word. That word is *love*.

Some will come through with their personalities intact, while others have just a brief message to let you know they've made it safely to the other side. Others come through to bring you comfort while you are still learning your lessons on the life plane.

They wish for us to understand the process and to be able to accept and understand the signs that we are receiving. For them, it's like learning a whole new language; and, they have many guides to help them understand this through their transition. It is now our turn to be skilled in this language, for it takes two to be able to understand the communication so that such messages can be received. By accepting the possibility, you open the door to the communication's energy that is already there. When you open your heart and accept the possibility that your loved one is trying to make connect with you; then, you are already connected at a certain level, for you have already created that link to your loved one on the other side.

I think it's also important to mention that the departed get great joy out of sending the signals and interrupting us in our daily lives. For some of them, it might be like a practical joke. For others, it could be from a deep yearning to relieve some of the suffering you may be going through. Their intentions may differ, but the results are the same: bringing love and understanding through is the objective of the signs.

Continue to talk to your loved ones, because they can surely hear you. Know that their loving essence will be around you for the continuation of your life. Often, they have reminded me that they do enjoy a good laugh, as this is one of the most healing methods available on the physical plane. They enjoy the energy and healing your experience, especially when you realize that something funny was caused by them.

If you want to be in contact with one of your loved ones, have love in your heart, laughter on your mind and sincerity in your purpose; and, you will receive the contact you have wished for.

On the other hand, if you wish to continue living out your life without any interaction with your loved ones or guides, this is also totally acceptable. They will have no interaction with you unless you ask for it and they will watch over you and watch you grow until it's your time to join them on the other side.

You have the opportunity to make your individual decision concerning communicating, contacting or understanding the signs from a loved one. Take it, for that opportunity is there to enjoy. Gain relief from the signs, learn from them, and teach them to others. Most importantly, give a sign back from your heart, for it will be accepted with more joy than you could ever imagine.

"We are not human beings on a spiritual journey.

We are spiritual beings on a human journey."

Pierre Teilhard de Chardin
1881- 1955
French philosopher and Jesuit Priest.

Part One
They are Always with You

ONE

Explanation of the Channeling Process

❦

Author's comments:

*W*hile writing this book, I thought it would be important to explain how the channeled information was acquired and translated. Many people are aware of the process in general, but I thought it would be interesting to hear it directly from their perspective. When I say "their", I mean my guides and teachers from the other side.

I have left this information intact so that you can try to understand the whole process. It seems more elaborate to me than what they explain, but that is just my perspective. I am on the receiving side; and, at times, it can be a challenge to stay connected for a great length of time. Although, I have noticed that the more I do it for longer periods of time, the easier it is to continue on for longer intervals.

The following is how they wished to present their perspective on the communication process:

It is our understanding that explaining the channeling process to your readers will enable them to see how this part of the book was completed.

First, we would like to introduce ourselves.

We are a group of guides, teachers and loved ones who have been working with Joseph throughout the years. He has shown an ability to interact with our side and to be able to transcribe our thoughts and messages. We have worked with him both physically and spiritually throughout his life. We have guided him through the ups and downs of his existence and we have been directly involved in many cases of supporting him as to a particular direction he has chosen. He and only he has made the decisions and directions in his life. We have been there to support, guide and love him throughout all his learning situations.

Some would have you think that we are just various energies and consciousness flowing in and around his structure, but we are more than that. We are conscious beings who have made it our purpose to intercede and help guide individuals on the physical plane.

Joseph was introduced to us as part of his courtship process of being chosen for the particular path that he entered into. From an early age, he was aware that we were interacting with him; and, we continued to support him, even when he did not acknowledge our existence.

We have noticed an intense change in the energies surrounding Joseph, which enable us to tap into him more easily and with more confidence. He has shown a great disregard for the fear that is associated around this process. Also, he has agreed to work with us on a daily basis in order for us to train and help him to develop his mediumistic skills. We wish to congratulate him on his effort with this book, as we have been waiting to bring this information to your plane for some time. His personal influence on the subject has melded quite well with our ideas and explanations; and, he has learned new knowledge while writing this book that he did not have prior to the beginning of this project.

We asked Joseph to communicate this particular knowledge, as we have seen a great need for it from individuals on your side and from individuals who have passed to our side.

The interaction between the two sides has been vast at times, and we wish to make it more accessible to everyone who wishes to open their hearts and think of the possibilities that they can achieve just by knowing that we exist.

Throughout time and in the recent past, we have set out to inform people on your plane about different topics. To accomplish this, we have used other people to submit our knowledge and insight. We have chosen these people because of their makeup, their spiritual essence and their ability to place their individual burdens to the side while knowing that the information coming through is for the greater will and it will help relieve suffering that many have experienced.

We understand that some people will discard the process that we will explain, but we are not interested in presenting scientific fact, as many will disregard some of the information for various reasons.

We see that there is a great wanting for information concerning one's essence and one's meaning in the transference of the soul from the physical plane to our plane.

So the process was begun sometime ago to collect information and to put it into a presentation that we would have transcribed through a medium. The information that follows in this book is meant to bring condolence, hope, love, and relief to the many who take advantage of the insights and learnings of this project.

As for the technological explanation of how a channel works, that is something that we can explain to a certain extent; but, at times, it may seem to be discombobulated.

We have analyzed the thought waves and mechanisms that Joseph's biological structure uses on a daily basis. Further, we try to interact with these thought patterns in order to mix our thoughts in with them so that he might understand the information that is coming from our side.

Once there was a general recognition of how Joseph's particular pattern works, we were able to intercede and stimulate certain mechanisms that alerted him of our presence. Over time, and with much patience and practice Joseph has learned to accept our invitations to communicate. He has trained himself to put his conscious focus to one side so that we may input data into his conscious mind for him to transcribe and to understand.

Joseph has been willing and able to learn this process over time, and we understand that it takes much energy for one to be able to continue to do this. We see that this method of communicating is much more efficient than using some of the signs you will read about in this book, as the information that we need for him to transfer is of such an amount that single, individual contacts would prohibit this process.

We can and will interact with others on the physical plane as long as you accept the conditions of this process. You must be open to the possibility of communication in this method. You must accept the responsibility that comes with transferring this knowledge; and, above all, you must want to be able to bring comfort and compassion to others around you.

The technical knowledge to interact between our side and your physical human being is something that has worked since time started. Some of you might have experienced it in other ways, such as through feelings, a sense of a presence or perhaps through so-called psychic ability. You should know that these mechanisms are built into your physiological structure and can be tapped into at will.

Some people developed the use of these capabilities at an early age, while others will not have the opportunity to experience these abilities at all. Many people will not wish to accept the fact that these aptitudes do exist on a large level throughout the physical plane and this non-acceptance will stagnate the communication effort between our side and yours.

With so many people not able to accept the possibility of this contact, we are limited to the amount of individuals who are able to communicate the vast knowledge and insights we need to pass along to humanity.

It is our view that the progress of the communication method is growing in certain circles and remains stagnant in others. We anticipate that by reading this information and gaining insight as to what can be, that we will not only relieve suffering but that we will instill hope, love and compassion. Also, we want people to realize that we are open to communicating with them on an individual basis and that we wish to invite them to join us in this contact.

TWO

No, You're not Crazy

❦

(Channeled from my guides)

*M*any times, when we try to contact your side, we are met with disbelief and uncertainty. We have done our homework. We have listened to your intentions. We have analyzed your ability to receive and understand the message and, yet, the sign is not picked up or accepted.

After the passing of a loved one, many people talk directly to the deceased about how they miss them, love them and wish they were still around. This opens up the channel for communicating with our side. You have set the intention by your thoughts and your actions to open a line of communication with your deceased loved one.

Our reaction is to go through the necessary protocol in order to teach your past loved one the dynamics of interacting with your side. This puts into motion a whole series of actions and investigations on how to best contact you.

Sometimes, the signs go unseen, as they might be confusing, mixed too well into the background of your daily lives; or, maybe just because you're preoccupied with other things on your mind.

But what we see is someone seeing a sign and trying to accept what they believe to be true: That a connection has occurred between their loved one on the other side and themselves. This is where disbelief and the uncertainty come into play. Most people are naturally skeptical of things that they cannot touch, see, feel or understand to be of a natural source. Even though they have set up the intention to communicate with the past love one, when the answer comes, they are still astonished as to its genuineness.

We have obviously picked the right time and location to gain your attention, as you do actually pick up on the sign. But, now you're physical, analytical mind begins to try to understand if this whole concept is actually possible. This is a natural state, as you're on the physical plane to learn and experience new growth opportunities. You wish to believe that the intention you had set out originally has now connected and you are actually receiving the sign that you have been waiting for.

The doubts and analytical thinking begin to confuse you, throw you off balance and make you wonder if you're starting to lose your grip on reality. Perhaps, you think it's just wistful thinking; or, maybe it's just a coincidence, as this could not possibly be happening. "This can't be real, they're dead." "Why is it still happening?" "Why did this particular event happen?"

It happened because you asked for it to happen. You might not have asked for a sign verbally, but you did through your emotions or your thoughts. You might have open lines of communication, where you wish there was still contact with the loved one who has passed.

We will discuss various methods on how we connect with your side later on in the book. They will vary from the simple sounds of someone's voice to the more complex meetings within a dream.

But the most important thing to remember is that *you're not losing your grip on reality*, that these events and signs that are appearing around you are actual communications from your loved ones on the other side. This communication method has been used since the beginning of human time.

You are not the first to experience these types of contact, nor will you be the last. You see, as spiritual beings, you are always in contact with the other side, as this is where you originally came from; and, this is where you'll return to. After you leave the physical plane through the transition called death, you will be able to connect with your loved ones who remain on the physical plane. As spiritual entities, you are connected to all those who are here with you and to others on the other side. You only think that you are limited by your physical being to be able to connect with others. Once you are free from limitations of your physical body, your consciousness and spirit are free to interact with many others at any time or place.

We just happen to choose a particular method that we think might gain your attention in the easiest and most efficient way. If you're thinking of a loved one and a favorite song of theirs comes on the radio, and it makes you think, "That was strange," than the message, the sign, was successful. The most important thing is not to doubt the sign when it comes across your path, as it has been intended for you to receive that communication at that particular time in that particular place. The fact that you pick it up and wonder about it is evidence that the communication was clear enough to stop you in your daily thoughts and to concentrate on what has just happened. We've grabbed your attention. Sometimes, people feel as though we've shaken you to attention. Sometimes the sign can be quite obvious.

Very often, we will have to repeat a sign multiple times before someone finally believes what they had thought in the first place, that it is a true contact with their loved one. We understand this and that is why we continue to give you a sign, even if you are having difficulty accepting it because of your doubts or fears.

At times, it can be quite comical, as you receive the sign and think to yourself, "Where did that come from?"

What happens next is that you usually begin to think about the event over and over throughout the following few days. Sometimes, one will confide in friends and family and tell them what has happened. Others will keep this information to themselves, as they're afraid of being ridiculed and called crazy. But, what people don't realize is that many many people have had the same type of experience and were made to feel exactly as you do when you try to figure out what is happening, what has happened and if it will happen again.

Don't think that you are alone in these circumstances, because millions of other people have experienced the same thing as you. This is the way that we try to communicate with you; and, at times, it can be subtle, while at other times, it can be quite obvious. Once you start to connect the dots, you'll begin to see a pattern of how this all works: Your thoughts about a past loved one, the sign coming through, how appropriate it might be for that time, how it relates to a current situation in your life or, perhaps, some insight that is needed to help resolve or deal with a particular problem .These are all reasons why we come to you.

Some people will have biological and physiological manifestations that occur to or around them. Those are not associated with us at all. There are various natural phenomena that can occur and manipulate a certain situation that we are not a source of. People with certain mental illnesses also have been associated with the phenomena of signs; but most often, this has just been an easy way to categorize something of the unknown.

Most of you living your daily lives, losing a loved one and wanting to connect with them once again will have the ability to receive the sign from our side; and, it is totally up to you whether you will accept the sign or let it pass by. Do not be shocked or frightened by this contact; let it open your heart and receive it with the love that was intended. Realize that your family, friends and associates have received similar signs - some privately, others talked about late at night.

The bottom line is to be happy and joyous that you have had the ability to pick up the communication that has been specifically prepared just for you. You are the main part of a successful contact attempt. Without your understanding and acceptance, that communication from your loved one will simply go by your consciousness and will never have the impact that it was intended to make.

Our intentions are to strengthen the loving bond that we have shared with you on the physical plane and continue to share with you. When we have passed, we can do this without communicating directly with you through the use of signs; but, we wish to have you experience the love and joy we get when connecting to you this way.

No, you are not crazy and thanks for accepting our invitation to say "Hello."

Author's comments:

When I have talked to people about the subject matter for this book and listened to their stories, there seemed to be a common thread. Initially, most of them thought that they might be imagining what was happing. I, too, have had this reaction and I should know better. We all experience doubt, because this is just a natural self-checking mechanism we all share. Knowing that millions of others believe in the concept of connecting to our departed loved ones brings some solace by recognizing that we are not alone in our experiences and that many others have actually received a sign.

THREE

Why do Our Loved Ones Come to Us?

❦

(Channeled from my guides)

There are many reasons why we try to contact you, once we have passed over. Right now, we will give you the general reasons; and, then, we will get into more detail about the exact meaning of this contact.

The obvious reason that we try to make contact with you is to let you know that our consciousness has survived the physical death of our body. Our spiritual entity is free from the confines of the physical plane. We are able to move about, think freely and act without restraint. This is quite new to us, when we arrive on this side; and, we wish to be able to let our loved ones know that we are okay and that we are actually still around. So the main reason of contact is simply to let you know that we exist.

One of the other reasons contact is sought with your side is to let you know that we continue to be involved and can interact with you throughout your whole life. Because we have crossed over does not mean that we have lost the ability to make emotional, mental or spiritual contact with you. We can be just as involved - or even more so - in your lives and your family's lives than if we were still physically there with you.

Obviously, our absence on the physical plane can be seen by the lack of our presence in your daily lives. However, we are still interested in how you progress throughout your life and how you are growing and learning as individuals.

We, too, miss our family, friends and colleagues just as you miss us. But, we must remind you that, from our perspective, we are not gone. Actually, we just have a different vantage point to interact with all of you.

It is our objective to be able to let our loved ones know that we can help them and comfort them during difficult times as well as celebrate the joys and happiness that they are experiencing. We are not physically there, but we have the ability to listen, to hear, and to feel the emotions that are expressed by our loved ones living on the physical plane.

By creating a sign and opening the avenues of communication, it is our intention that our loved ones will realize that we have not died and that they can be in contact with us as long as they wish.

Do not think that our lives now reflect totally around your daily living, as we also have continuing lessons to learn. Our time is used to analyze past experiences and to learn the new experiences of our current existence. So we are not breathing down your neck constantly and trying to interfere with your life's progress. We actually have our own life to continue, but it is on our side.

By making the connection and opening the line of communication, we give you the option of continuing to connect with us and continuing to communicate with us throughout the time you have left on your physical plane. It brings us great joy when you realize that life continues after the so-called change called death, that you will never be alone, and that someday you'll be with us again. When we see people understanding this knowledge, it brings us closer to them in knowing that we are all truly connected - our side and your side - and that we are only divided by a brief thought or a simple sign.

At other times, we try to connect with you to bring you a message of hope and encouragement and to let you know that you have support from our side. In order to help you in a certain situation, we will also try to come through and contact you if there is an urgent message that you need to understand. But, most of the time, it is simply to say hello, to let you know that we are still around and that we still love you very much.

Always with You

While I was giving a mediumistic reading to a twenty-something-year-old gentleman, to whom I will refer as Chris (not his real name), some significant information came through that relates to the information that Spirit introduced us to in the previous section.

Chris had lost his father, who died at an early age, two years back. His dad first brought through validating information to prove who he was and then talked to Chris about some little things that were going on during his life and to show that he was still there to support him. He mentioned that Chris was never alone and that he would always be there for him. He mentioned that he would present a sign when he was around.

The following is an exact transcript of the reading given to Chris by me. It took place about six or seven years ago through Instant Messenger and I saved it in order to gauge my mediumistic development at that time. To protect his privacy, I have changed the online name that Chris uses.

I have moved to the section where his father begins to give us information so that we might recognize exactly who he is. Some personal identification that came through before this section is left out to protect Chris's privacy. Afterwards, we moved to sections concerning a show of support: not being alone, always being there for Chris, and knowing what is happening in his daily life.

The most touching part of the reading came towards the end, when the father discussed how he would be with his son as he grows older. The visualization that the father gave to me and I described to Chris brought tears of joy to my eyes, because I could feel the extreme love the father had for his son.

This is one of the wonderful side effects of being a medium. We get to share in the emotions and joy that are brought through and communicated from the other side to ours. To this day, I can still see the father walking with his son and the joy of love emanating from this connection.

Readingsbyjh: I'm hearing colt 45, lol
Readingsbyjh: so I thought beer or a gun, lol
(Chris)xxxxx: lol could be both with him
Readingsbyjh: maybe that's why I heard it that way then, lol

(Chris)xxxxx:	lol probably, he has a weird sense of humor
Readingsbyjh:	he just took something off a shelf and is showing it to me
(Chris)xxxxx:	can you tell what it is?
Readingsbyjh:	like a framed something or something that opens up
Readingsbyjh:	he is opening it and trying to show me...
Readingsbyjh:	it could be a weapon
(Chris)xxxxx:	he had one, didn't carry it though
Readingsbyjh:	I think it might be up on something. It's up on a wall
Readingsbyjh:	this is weird...did he shoot black powder
(Chris)xxxxx:	hmm...not sure
Readingsbyjh:	I think its something in a frame
Readingsbyjh:	he is showing me a long barrel gun and putting something in the barrel
Readingsbyjh:	maybe cleaning a shot gun or something.
Readingsbyjh:	I'll see if I get some more info
(Chris)xxxxx:	possible, he had a shot gun too, it's still here in the house. He has a black powder gun from the civil war period hanging on a wall in a frame
Readingsbyjh:	that's it then, the frame, the black powder gun
(Chris)xxxxx:	yeah it looks like that, one of those framed cases hanging on the wall
Readingsbyjh:	thanks for pulling it together....
(Chris)xxxxx:	no thank you lol
(Chris)xxxxx:	lol that's gotta be it...hi daddy ;)
Readingsbyjh:	he took off his cap and tipped it toward you....lol
Readingsbyjh:	let's see who else is around....you're open, so it helps out

(Chris)xxxxx: ok

Readingsbyjh: I'm hearing the name Frank

(Chris)xxxxx: living or past?

Readingsbyjh: either, I just heard the name

(Chris)xxxxx: I had an uncle frank

Readingsbyjh: passed?

(Chris)xxxxx: yes

Readingsbyjh: that could be him validating he is around

Readingsbyjh: do you have a Helen who has passed?

Readingsbyjh: and she was elderly

(Chris)xxxxx: I had an aunt Helen, deceased, yes elderly.

(Chris)xxxxx: my grandmother's sister was Helen

Readingsbyjh: this woman is now clapping

Readingsbyjh: like with a sing along

(Chris)xxxxx: lol

(Chris)xxxxx: it is a party

Readingsbyjh: I've seen it before, lol

Readingsbyjh: she is waving to you

(Chris)xxxxx: lol hi aunt Helen

Readingsbyjh: throwing a kiss and waving bye. She is stepping back

Readingsbyjh: they're all together

(Chris)xxxxx: having a blast I'm sure

Readingsbyjh: *they say "don't feel alone"*

Readingsbyjh: *"we're all with you"*

Readingsbyjh: *"just call us"*

(Chris)xxxxx: lol what's the phone number?

Readingsbyjh: *they seem to have their own things to do, but want you to know they are there for you anytime*

(Chris)xxxxx: tell them thank you, I appreciate it

(Chris)xxxxx: and I love them

Readingsbyjh: one of the guys said, lol *"call us collect"*, lol

(Chris)xxxxx: LOL

Readingsbyjh: They are talking about a sister

(Chris)xxxxx: I have three sisters, two are still here

Readingsbyjh: they said *they're all here for you and your sister*

(Chris)xxxxx: that makes sense, it's me and my little sister here, my older one is distant from the family

Readingsbyjh: well they're showing/validating *that they know what is going on in your life and support you*

(Chris)xxxxx: thanks

Readingsbyjh: *they said they know what you're going through and will try to help*

(Chris)xxxxx: tell them thank you, I appreciate that

Readingsbyjh: they want to share with you their knowledge

Readingsbyjh: *so they will be there to help you*

Readingsbyjh: *and they wish the best for you*

(Chris)xxxxx: tell them all I love them ;)

Readingsbyjh: *"and we'll try to make things happen a little faster"*

(Chris)xxxxx: lol good

Readingsbyjh: *"you do your part, we'll do ours"*

(Chris)xxxxx: deal ;)

Readingsbyjh: is there a situation going on

Readingsbyjh: that would affect you or your sister?

(Chris)xxxxx: yeah

Readingsbyjh: they said something about how she is handling it....

(Chris)xxxxx: ok...makes sense to me

Readingsbyjh: they said be a comfort to her

Readingsbyjh: she'll appreciate it

(Chris)xxxxx: will do, as always

Readingsbyjh: they said that bob says hi

(Chris)xxxxx: lol hi bob

Readingsbyjh: do you know him? I'm curious

(Chris)xxxxx: yeah lol I know him

Readingsbyjh: great...well tell me, I'm in the dark here, lol

(Chris)xxxxx: lol if it's the bob I'm thinking of, old friend from school who passed away, he was known to just say hi in the middle of other peoples' conversations

Readingsbyjh: Your dad's leaving, nice exit...they sometimes do something funny. This time they were all in the back of a convertible race car and turned and drove away...all of them packed in the car...left a smoke trail, lol

(Chris)xxxxx: lol that's gotta be dad, he had a convertible race car

Readingsbyjh: he is still here

Readingsbyjh: I feel his love for you

Readingsbyjh: *he said to listen for him he will be around*

Readingsbyjh: he slapped your back

(Chris)xxxxx: I do everyday...lol

Readingsbyjh: and he whispers in your ear

Readingsbyjh: listen to his guidance

(Chris)xxxxx: always have, always will

(Chris)xxxxx: doesn't mean I follow, but I listen lol

Readingsbyjh: he walks with you and has his arm around your shoulders

Readingsbyjh: he says you're a good kid

(Chris)xxxxx: lol

(Chris)xxxxx: I always say that, I'm the good kid lol

Readingsbyjh: he will be with you as you grow

Readingsbyjh: and will see you some day

(Chris)xxxxx:	I look forward to it
Readingsbyjh:	he is shaking your hand,
Readingsbyjh:	you look older, though, means a long life I guess, lol
(Chris)xxxxx:	lol great
Readingsbyjh:	he is going one way and you the other....
(Chris xxxxx)	that was a nice visit. I like the ending too. Nice, very nice. I feel a peaceful warmth

As I related to Chris about his father walking with him and putting his arm around his shoulders, I was shown an adult male standing next to a male in his twenty's. I could feel that these two men were Chris and his father. They were walking down a path and talking to each other as the father put his arm around Chris's shoulder. He was saying to tell Chris that he would be with him as he grows and walks down his own path of life. What he meant was that he would be with his son throughout the milestones of his life.

I could see Chris getting married, having a child and other various events of his upcoming life. As the two continued to walk down the path, Chris became more like an older adult as he reached these various milestones. His father was still walking by his side, signifying that he was with him throughout these times. As the two continued down the path, I could see Chris beginning to lose his hair when he began to reach middle age. At the same time, I could see his father, who had been a young, robust adult, starting to shrink a little and walk slightly hunched over. As Chris began to move past middle age, I noticed that his father was much more frail and had begun to walk with a cane. Tears began to fill my eyes as I understood what was happening and how magnificent and significant this vision truly was.

Chris's father has shown to me that he would be with Chris from the time he passed over, throughout his son's entire life, until he reached old age.

Even though Chris's father had passed and was on the other side, he would walk with his son down his son's path to help support him, guide him and be with him to enjoy all the milestones throughout his life.

The feelings associated with the vision that showed me how a loved one, who has passed can still be with us through our daily lives are almost indescribable. The love and support were extraordinary. There is no doubt that you never walk alone, for you have many loved ones and guides with you throughout your entire life.

I can relate to this communication between a father and son, because I lost my loving father at a very early age. This particular reading gave me such insight as to how our loved ones can be around us and experience the events of our lives, even though they have passed.

I thank Chris's father for showing me that beautiful visual and letting me experience all the love that surrounded it, so that I might use it as an example in this book. I feel certain that many people will gain wonderful insight and healing from this story, just as I have in my own life.

Joe Higgins

Part Two
How Do They Do It?

FOUR
Methods Unlimited

❦

(Channeled from my guides)

*T*he reason that these specific methods of contact were chosen was to give you an idea on the variety of ways that we can go about trying to communicate with you. We have noticed that a majority of people possess the ability to recognize signs once they have understood these explanations. It is not our intention to try to make the connections more difficult than they can be.

We like to use familiar things that you interact with in your daily lives. It is also our intention to relate to the vast majority of people who have witnessed contact from these methods.

Depending on the individual, specific methods may be used, and they include the phenomenon of apparitions. These are used in specific circumstances when a loved one wishes to appear physically before the ones they left behind. At times, this method can create intense feelings, including happiness, joy and - on certain occasions - anxiety and stress.

It is not the intention of the past loved one to create unease for the recipient of the sign. There are at times when a physical appearance may disrupt the relaxed atmosphere at the time of contact. We understand that if you awake in the middle of the night and see a loved one standing in your room, it has the possibility of being intimidating and causing stress to you.

On these occasions, the loved one has disregarded some of the limitations we have put on contact and continued on with their express will to show themselves. We do try, however, to intercede to make your acceptance of these appearances more relaxed and comforting.

Every individual spiritual entity has free will as to the actions and responsibilities that they are to take. When the spirit loved one decides to make an appearance, we feel the spirit is doing this out of intense emotional joy so as to be able to be recognized and accepted.

While we prefer to coach the newly arriving spirit as to the various methods that are available and accepted, at times your loved ones can be a little impatient, and sometimes downright pushy. We are here to guide them and give them instruction. However, in the end, they will make the ultimate decision as to how they wish to connect with you.

Many times, people have a close relationship with the natural surroundings of the physical plane. Within these boundaries are methods of contact that can be arranged to show a sign. We have the ability to intercede in the action of the animal world as well as with plants and the weather. If someone would recognize a sign more easily through the action of an animal, or a significant flower or breeze, then this would be implemented in the choice of contact.

We are not limited as to the methods of contact and we have vast, interacting abilities within the physical plane.

FIVE

Smells

❧

(Channeled from my guides)

Author's Comments:

J *am sure that many of you have been going about your daily lives when suddenly a scent appears to you which reminds you instantly of a past loved one. "Is it my imagination or where did that come from," are common thoughts that run through our minds when something like this happens. Then, we look around and realize that there is no source for that smell to attribute it to. "How can this be?" we ask. As soon as we begin to realize that this scent we just picked up reminds us of our passed love one, then an overwhelming calm and joy will come with that recognition.*

You see, acceptance is the first step in order to understand and continue to receive signs in this manner. If we simply disregard these strange aromas as just coincidences, then, they will stop; and, a new avenue for signs will be attempted. Accepting signs will allow more to come our way and our lives will be enriched by our knowing our love ones are around us and just wanting to say "hi.".

My spirit guides have provided some insight into this type of connection and I would like to share this with you.

Trust our intention to give you insight into the many different ways that we use to communicate with you. One of these options is by the use of scent or smell.

We know that you have had many experiences with using your sense of smell as it is quite appropriate for our intentions. By this, we mean it is easy for us to get through the barrier to gain your attention by focusing our signal, as you like to call them, on one of your senses.

For your species, the sense of smell is very strong, and it can be used to remind you of past events and times, as well as current things going on around you. Therefore, it is with great ease that we can tap into this sense and use it to gain your attention.

As with your other senses, this one can be used while the subject is going about his/her daily life. We don't have to make a blatant sign to the recipient. Just a whiff of perfume or perhaps the smell of a fatherly cigar will suffice. Candles, perfumes, or the scent of a man or woman as well as hundreds of other recognizable aromas can lead to the remembrance of one of your love ones who has passed.

How easy it is to forget one's name when you are on this side. It is so random to be recognized by one common term: a name. We find it much easier to recognize someone from a variety of aspects, such as the personality, traits, achievements, and the smells related to them. So, we have found it to be much more appropriate to contact your side with the easiest possible signs of which the sense of smell is one.

For some people, different smells produce different reactions. For a daughter, it may be the smell of a deceased mother's perfume. For a father, it could be the smell of his daughter's freshly shampooed hair. For others, it could be the smell of a fresh wax job on someone's antique car.

We have found that the easiest way to get someone's attention to the sense of smell is to have the person remember a fond moment with the loved one who has passed. So it might be smells associated with getting ready for work or perhaps someone's going off to school or even just the smell of the fresh air coming through the window on a quiet summer's night.

Depending upon their individual experiences, each person will have different memories from which we can draw. Their departed loved ones will pick the memories that they think will remind those on your plane of their loved ones on our plane. You see, we have the ability to feel how our love ones remember us.

This is when we can tap into specific smells that we know will generate a response from the person who we try to contact. At times, this might be subtle and brief and, at other times, it can be quite obvious and lingering.

We know the response that we are looking for and we plan accordingly. However, people often have a tendency to overlook these signs and to go about their daily lives. However, the use of the sense of smell rings deep in one's heart to the point where many people will actually stop and analyze what is happening. This is when the spark of connection is ignited. From here, we are open to communication at a very easy level.

The response that we have seen from flooding your senses with fond memories of us is a great thrill to us. We can feel the closeness and love that you have generated for us at this time, this moment. Through smell, we see a well-focused connection between individuals and their loved ones. It is personal and convincing, as no one else can interpret this connection or understand it as well as the recipient of the sense.

Later, and throughout the book, we will talk more about connecting to you through the use of smells. But, remember for now that the odd scent that you sense drifting toward you might be the sign that you have asked for, as we are cognitive of what it takes to connect with you.

Stop and Smell the Coffee

It always fascinates me when something wonderful happens directly to me. "Something" is the term we all use to describe a sign we don't understand. Therefore, I still use that term when describing a sign that comes through from the other side.

This particular event happened a couple of months after my mother passed to spirit. My sister had received a sign the night of my mothers wake, so I was not totally surprised by what happened. However, it did make me smile with that warm inner feeling one gets when one is deeply touched.

That evening, I went out to dinner with a close friend of mine, who had met my mother a few years before she passed. She and my mother got along very well and enjoyed each other's company. This woman was open to the whole idea of contact – or, I should say the possibility of something like that. However, she still had major reservations. When I refer to "reservations" and "open to the idea", it means that she, like many of us, is either a little scared by the whole subject or that she might have conflicting thoughts because of her religious upbringing.

Still, she was a good sport about listening to my many stories concerning some of the mediumistic readings I had given to others.

After dinner at a local restaurant, we decided to head back to my house to watch a movie and relax. It was late spring and I had left all the windows in the house closed, since it was a little cool but not cold enough to have the heat on. When we arrived, we entered through the front door and went into the kitchen to put some leftovers into the refrigerator. We had to walk through the dining room in order to access the kitchen.

We might have been in the kitchen for less than three minutes. As we entered the dining room, I immediately smelled the most robust scent of freshly brewed coffee that I had smelled since my mother's passing. This was not just the aroma of a cup of coffee that one might have with dinner. Instead, this was the smell you would encounter on a holiday, when a giant urn would be set up to serve a large group.

My mother loved to entertain and she loved her coffee. At the end of her life, she was barely able to consume anything; but, she always requested a cup of coffee, which brought a smile to her face despite the pain and suffering she was enduring.

As I continued to walk through the dining room, which had been the scene of many a holiday gathering, I stopped myself from asking my friend, "Do you smell that coffee?" I wanted to get an untainted answer from her without any suggestion from me about what was actually taking place.

Consequently, I just stopped, turned to her and said, "Do you find anything different?" This could have referred to any number of things – from the furniture to the wall paper to the next room coming up or even the kitchen we had just been in. She stopped, looked at me and said in the most surprised voice, "Oh my God. It smells like coffee." The whole room was filled with this delicious aroma and she looked at me and asked where it came from. I told her it must be from my mother, because that would have been a perfect sign to let me know she was around and still with me.

It is important to mention that neither one of us had coffee at dinner. I had not had any in about two years, nor was there even a bean in the house. All the windows and doors had been shut tight and there wasn't any smell on our clothes. I smiled at her while she experienced this true sign from the other side. Although her first instinct was to try to dismiss what was happing, she just couldn't. She was both in a state of belief and disbelief at the same time, if that is even possible.

We then continued to the living room. I had a big smile on my face and my friend had a look of total awe. She tried to analyze the whole thing but could not come up with any other reason for the occurrence. As we sat in the living room for a few minutes, I mentioned to her that I bet if one went back into the dining room right now, the smell would be gone. She said, "That would be impossible, because the scent of coffee lingers for quite some time. I laughed and said, "Go and see." She immediately got up from her chair, walked back into the dining room and let out a gasp as she said "Joe, it's gone, totally gone." To check this out for myself, I also walked over to witness the fact that the scent of coffee had actually left the room.

To this day, my friend continues to be amazed by what happened that night; and, her witnessing that sign with me brought me great joy, since so many times these signs happen to us while we are alone.

Joe Higgins

SIX

Sounds

❧

(Channeled from my guides)

Sound is an interesting aspect of our communication, or "sign", as you like to call it. It can be very precise and also very subtle at the same time. We don't need to be able to read your intentions in order to communicate with you through this manner, as all we need to do is play a few notes and we have your immediate attention.

You see, sounds in your existence are related to a basic survival mechanism. Therefore, it is an essential part of your being. We understand that there are some people who do not have this sense but that they do have other abilities that make up for it. We have seen that communicating to you through the sense of sound can be very gratifying for those who are receiving the message. There is so much emotion related to different sounds and vibrations that they can strike a remembrance of a loved one more easily than some other senses that we have referred to in this book.

For example, Someone's particular romantic song that they shared with a loved one would be an intimate sound that they would remember immediately. On the other hand, a large bang or noise might gain the person's attention immediately, because it did not fit the pattern of the sounds that were occurring naturally at the time. If someone hears a bang or crash, their attention to what they are doing ceases in order to find out what is happened. There could be a knock on the door to let you know that we are here. But at other times, the sounds could be more profound and intimate, such as when we manipulate certain devices in order for a predetermined sound to come through. An example might be a song from an electrical device.

Music could be a separate category to the main objective of sound in this chapter. It lends itself to a whole variety of different aspects for communicating with your side. Our music and your music have similarities, as they bring back sweet memories of past times and connections to friends and loved ones. One of the reasons why we use music in order to awaken your attention is that it is built deeply within your senses of remembrance, it can be tapped into very easily and it is often recognizable in a split second.

General sounds, such as banging, rapping or pinging, are used to grab your attention away from one of the daily activities you are involved in at that time. These may be used in the beginning of a connection in the communication process, but, not in themselves, as communication method. However, these sounds have been used in the past and will be used again as direct communications with the receiver. That is something that we do not want to focus on right now, as it can become complicated and requires much more definition and explanation.

We can access the sounds that you need to hear to gain your attention through different methods, including but not limited to: musical instruments; electrical devices; natural sounds from nature; and even sounds related to events, such as the Fourth of

July. We might even employ sounds associated with graduations, birthdays and celebrations.

Have you ever been driving down the road and a song comes on the radio to remind you of your loved one who has passed? Perhaps, you were just thinking of that person. It is not a coincidence. You might be the only one who actually hears the song, or it might be heard by many others. But, it is a sign from us that your connection to your loved one was just opened by your thoughts, and is being responded to by that particular song.

When you recognize that song, it is like a wave from your loved one to you. It's a brief moment between the two of you. It can be very intimate or it might be shared with friends. Groups, as well as individuals, are allowed to hear the sounds and connections, as when a loved one passes. It not only affects the individual, but such a passing can affect a group of friends or family at the same time. So sounds have also been made available in the group setting in order for more than one individual to receive the sign at one time. We can be very efficient in connecting with you, and this is something that we enjoy. It makes us work.

At other times, something as subtle as a rain drop of water, a drip from a faucet, or the sound of waves pounding the beach are used. These particular sounds will also remind you of a loved one who has passed. It is not the sound that we have created; it's just that we have enhanced the sound and how it is recognized by you. This means that if you have fond memories of walking down a beach with a loved one and listening to the ocean crash against the beach, your loved one could pick that particular scene in that particular environment in order to be connected to it. In this case, you might be flooded with thoughts of the sounds of the ocean hitting the beach in order for you to remember the special moments you spent with your loved one.

In this case, beach sounds are used as a remembrance and a connecting factor in order to open the lines of communication. As long as the sound directly or indirectly opens your attention to the loved one on the other side, then the sign is a success. It's like opening a gate and allowing the flow of communication to start between the individual and the one who has passed.

It is all about gaining attention. It's all about putting the emphasis on something that will interrupt you from your daily thinking patterns and have you focus in on the memory and feelings in connection with the past loved one. Some of these signs are misinterpreted, as they can bring general happiness or even grief to the person receiving the hint. It is important for us to have you understand that our intentions are to bring comfort, peace, and serenity to those receiving these signs. If one becomes upset or does not understand why something is happening, this also brings grief to our side, as it is not our intention to create this type of turmoil in the loved one's life.

That is why it is important for you, the people who read this book to understand that all the communications and signs that we present to you are assets - to bring relief from suffering and grief and to help open your hearts to your loved ones and to remind you that your loved ones are still here for you.

So the whole process can be very simple and complex at the same time. It is how well you understand the process that will make it easier for you when the signs are communicated to you. It is important to realize that these signs are meant as a way for you to understand that life goes on after the so-called stage of death. This also means that you'll be able to communicate with your loved ones when your time has come to move onto the next phase of your life.

So if you are ever daydreaming and a sound comes to you that reminds you of a loved one, it is not from lack of effort from our side, but it is a well-tuned effort at communication to let you understand that you are never alone and that your loved ones are always around and can help you in times of need.

Someday, if you hear the sound of an opera or perhaps the beating of a drum, music from a past concert, wind chimes blowing in the breeze, whispers in your ear or any vibration that brings your attention to your loved one, it has all been a well- orchestrated event that has been enabled for us to reach your consciousness.

Author's comments:

In our lives, the extensive use of sound has become a strong way for us to relate and to remember our past and interactions with our friends and family. Events, music and nature are a few ways that sound can bring out emotional responses from us. We often relate a particular sound or sounds to one person due to the familiarities that accrued when they were around.

Music seems to play a large part in connecting to us. Maybe it is because we tend to be separated from our conscience minds for brief moments when we listen to it, thus giving those on the other side the opportunity to connect. Music not only relaxes us and creates a good environment for contact, but it can distract us enough from our daily activities to respond to a sign.

Listen to the music

After being widowed for about two years, I had recently met a man who I really liked. We talked on the phone for a while and went out together a couple of times, so the relationship was very new. While on the phone one day, he asked me if I wanted to go see Fleetwood Mac in concert; and, I, in turn, asked him if he would accompany me to a friend's wedding. These events were not to happen for at least another month; so, although the relationship was new, we were making "long term" plans.

While driving later in the day, I began to panic, asking myself, "What did you just do?" I thought I had to be crazy for making plans for a month away, when we really did not know each other. Although I felt ready to move on with my life, the thought of a new relationship after being married for twenty-five years, was downright scary. Doubt and confusion began to creep into my brain. Although it sounds crazy, I began "talking" to my deceased husband, asking him for help with all of the questions I had running through my brain. "Is he really a nice guy?" "Is he good for me?" "Is this the right thing to do?" "What do you suggest?" I remember thinking, "I wish you could tell me what to do; I'm scared."

The radio was on in the car; and, at that moment, my husband's favorite song by Matchbox Twenty came on the radio. I remember thinking, "There you are." He loved all kinds of music, and was always listening to something. Hearing his favorite song at that moment, made me smile to myself; and, I felt somewhat comforted. However, it was the song that played right after the first one, which absolutely let me know he was there, listening and answering my questions. It was a Fleetwood Mac song! I knew without a doubt that he had heard me *and was using music, a medium that he loved so much, to answer my questions. He was letting me know that everything was alright, that it was OK to move on with this relationship and my life.*

Just in case I thought that the two songs were a coincidence, after running my errands, I returned to my car about an hour later. Playing on the radio was a Fleetwood Mac song and right after that, a Matchbox Twenty song. He was making sure that I definitely got his answers to my questions. It could not have been any more obvious. As I thanked him for answering me, I had tears in my eyes. Getting that sign made me feel so much better, less confused, and at peace with all of the changes happening in my life.

Nina M.

SEVEN

Electricity

❦

(Channeled from my guides)

*O*ne of the ways that we enjoy trying to make contact with you is through the electrical process that works on your plane. We realize that it can become very technical on how we can manipulate the signal between the electrical source and the outlet. So we do not wish to overburden you with the finer technical details of this process. We will, however, give you some background that you could use at a later time.

Electrical energy that is stored near the source can be manipulated easily with our thoughts. This is to say that we can change the output of a particular source in order to get the response we are looking for. In layman's terms, this means that we can make a light go on or off and perhaps make something flash, turn radios on, cause static in a connection or otherwise disrupt the normal flow of electrical impulses.

We use this manipulation in order to gain your attention; and, at times, it is the easiest manner to achieve this. If one is in deep thought and we wish to contact you in order to present a sign that we are around, we have found that by disrupting an electrical source and creating that sign we can grab your attention immediately. This is what we are trying to achieve.

Electricity is used in so many components on your plane of existence, and it is readily available to many whom we are trying to contact. So it is one of our most effective means of communication. One does not have to be in a deep meditation mode. One does not have to be thinking about us, and one does not even have to be cognizant of anything about our side. Just the fact that the change in electrical impulse can create an immediate reaction from someone is enough for us to use this method.

We find it easier with some people than others, such as if someone is used to loud music or sounds. This is something that's easily manipulated to get a response. Others notice subtle changes in temperature, lighting, or even the sound of an air conditioner. We can regulate the energy flow to any of these devices; and, by doing so, we can manipulate the range that they fall into. Some people can pick up on the subtle change, while others need a more drastic result.

We have worked with many different elements in products on your plane; and, depending on the individual, we decide on which manner is the easiest for us to transmit a sign so that the loved one will notice it with the least amount of effort.

Any electrical activity that surrounds a person can be changed or manipulated in order to get the result that is wanted. An example of this is that electric static from a carpet will cause a reaction to the human body. Sometimes, it can be a visual or audio reaction, as in the blinking of a light bulb or the sound of the chimes of the doorbell. We have used all of these and many more.

Consequently, it really depends on the individual we are trying to contact. We try to find the best way that they will pick up this information without having that person try to explain it as everyday stimulus.

Turning lights on and off is one of our favorites, because it's the easiest to recognize for you; and, the results are often immediate and convincing. We have also been able to make toasters pop, refrigerator lights go on and off, vacuum cleaners start on their own, and power tools to turn on or malfunction, as well as other everyday products that one would find in one's household. Remember, we are trying to get your attention; so, we want to use something that you're familiar with and something that will stand out from the ordinary when it does happen.

We manipulate this electricity in order to get your response. By doing it at certain times of the day or when you're preoccupied, we make the effect larger than it would ordinarily be.

Not to say that it is easy all the time. There are many instances when we use various electrical signs around one in order to connect with them, and none are picked up by the person we are trying to contact. Some people do not notice the signs or they wish them away and still others will find any excuse for the reason that the phenomenon has occurred.

But we can be persistent, especially when someone has asked for a sign from their loved one. In this case, we will try multiple attempts in order to achieve the contact that the loved one has asked for. If the results are not reached within a certain period of time, other means would be tried, such as smells, sounds and various interacting solutions.

When a person asks for a sign from their love one, we all work together to help enable the process to work properly. We help the loved one who has passed decide which is the best avenue to try to connect with their loved ones still on the physical plane, and this sets the whole process into play. The actions that have been requested by loved ones who are still alive on the physical plane are a powerful force that opens the connection to our side.

We can ask questions and achieve results from the findings, depending on individual characteristics of each person. This means if someone is used to using a particular product or device, the probability of the person recognizing the sign increases, as it most likely would come through one of those sources. For the husband who has used power tools throughout his life, and it is of a particular interest to him, we might use one of those devices to send a sign to the surviving wife, in order for her to recognize that the sign is indeed from her husband. This way, where the sign is coming from leaves little confusion to the partner or loved one who is left alive on the physical plane.

Author's comments:

It seems that electricity is simple for them to manipulate and easy for us to recognize when a sign occurs using this method. It really gives them access to us as we go about our daily lives, surrounded with electrical devices in our homes, workplaces, and even out in nature, where we are accompanied by our cell phones and musical devices. It makes sense they would choose to use electrical tools to get our attention. Back in time, perhaps they used other methods more often; but, in our day and age, electrical manipulation is one sure way to get our attention quickly.

Lights are on; anyone home?

This next story has to do with contact that I had with my deceased mother. My mother had come to me on various occasions with information to validate who was coming through and letting me know that it was, indeed, she who was in contact with me.

When it first happened, I didn't think it was truly possible; because, I know that when someone close to a medium tries to come through, we naturally wonder if it's our own mind, expectations or perhaps just wishful thinking that it is indeed that close friend or family member. The first time she came through to me, I was sitting with a friend who was working on the computer. While I was organizing some paperwork, I mentioned to that person that I thought my mother was coming through but that I wasn't sure. I didn't know how to confirm it, so my mother began to bring through some evidential information concerning the person I was with that only the two of them would have known. When pieces of information came through for the other person and they were able to confirm them, I began to think that perhaps I truly was in contact with my mother. This led me to believe that I really could separate my own analyzing and feelings from the communication methods that they were using on the other side. Finally, my mother mentioned that she really enjoyed the blue outfit that my friend had bought. At this point, my friend stopped working on the computer, turned to me with a surprised face and said, "Joe, that outfit is outside in my car right now." I replied, "Well, I guess my mom really likes it." Then, we both began to laugh and realized that we had just experienced a special moment with a passed love one.

Once in a while, if there was something on my mind, or if I have had an issue around me that needed verification, my mother would tap in to help me with some insight and then be off on her way. One evening, I was in my bedroom and the bathroom door was open. I felt my mother's presence around me and, at that exact time, the light above the sink started to blink two or three times. I amusingly asked my mother if that was going to be her new sign to let me know when she's around. The light flashed on and off. I laughed and said, "Fine. That just makes it very easy." A little bit of information came through that evening having to do with some particular situation. It was nothing of major importance but something that was probably just on my mind.

Over the next couple of months, the situation repeated itself several times. Sometimes, I would ask her to help me with decisions I was trying to make; and, at other times, my mom would come to me and give me some information or just to say hello. All the connections were preceded by the blinking of the light above the sink two or three times.

These communications have been witnessed by others, since they became quite regular. Over a few months, we used to laugh and say that it's better than using the phone. One evening, as I was preparing to go out, the light flashed a couple times and I knew a message from Mom was about to come through. On this particular evening I was in a little bit of a rush to attend an event and didn't have much time to make contact in that usual location – the bathroom.

Later that evening, when I returned home, I remember thinking about some concerns that I was having over the previous few weeks. Like most people, At times, I have my doubts about how all this works, and that concern does slip into my consciousness now and then about the concepts and possibilities that exist. However, this time it was different; because, this time I had a dilemma and the dilemma was *whether this was truly my mother coming through and notifying me by using electricity and a light as the sign. If it was not she, then there was a possibility that it was a wiring problem with that fixture.*

I'd been thinking about this possibility in the back of my mind and had actually begun to worry about it earlier that day. We all have things on our minds and an issue like this was not something that I needed. When I had mentioned these concerns to a friend of mine, she agreed that there could be a problem. Although my friend had witnessed some of the information coming through on other evenings, she asked me what I was going to do.

I decided to go directly to the source. I opened up and asked for mother to come through and show me a sign, because I needed to know if it was truly she or if I was to have to call an electrician the next morning. I told my mother that I did believe it was she; but, if I was wrong, the house could burn down. Partially joking, I said, "If it really is you and there is no problem with the fixture, then it still will cost me a couple of hundred bucks to have it checked out."

I had no sooner finished asking that question then the light blinked ten times and then stopped - and it has not blinked since!

I immediately thanked my mother for coming through and relieving the anxiety I had about a possible malfunctioning electrical fixture. Then, I laughed and thanked her for saving me a few hundred dollars. As a result, when she now wants to come through, she can come through directly; and, I don't need to have a physical sign. I also thanked my mom for relieving me of my doubts about her trying to connect with me.

It is amazing how spirits will interact with us as they listen and try to understand what is the easiest, most efficient and least stressful way to come through to us. In my mother's contact with me, using an electrical fixture is a perfect example on how they can adapt to connecting with us if we are willing to communicate back with them with our intentions.

Joe Higgins

EIGHT

Objects

❦

(Channeled from my guides)

*O*bjects are an interesting way for us to communicate with you. At times, it seems that you are directly connected to a physical object or presence that gives you a hint of that connection that you're looking for from the other side. We see that at times. The sense of smell is fooled by age or confused with all the aromas in your living space. Perhaps, your hearing isn't as good as it used to be from working in a factory or because of a decline due to age or injury. Those are some of the reasons why we pick other ways of communicating with you. One of these is through objects.

An object can be composed of solid matter, such as something that takes up a particular space, something that might be more fluid or something that will stand out. We use anything to make you take notice and recognize that we are trying to connect with you. We've seen many examples of how people accept our signs; and, depending on the individual, we will decide what the best method is to contact you. You all have had examples of objects that brought you fond memories, as well as reminding you of loved ones who have passed to our side.

These objects could be family heirlooms. They could be a recent gift or an object that is presented to you, which reminds you of the person you were thinking about. All of these methods and more are utilized with the recognition and sense you gain from a particular object. We don't necessarily pick the object; what we do is react to the signs and intentions you send to us.

If someone is reminded of a family member who drove a big, black Cadillac or, perhaps, had a coin collection or loved to work with flowers; then, these are the objects that we would use to gain your attention. Other times, it could be a ring of significant value, a card one had received, a handwritten letter or a small token of one's appreciation. There are literally hundreds of different objects that can be presented to you for you to recognize that a sign has arrived from one of your loved ones.

Different individuals will accept different objects, depending on the relationship to the one who is being contacted. Therefore, a baseball bat might mean nothing to one person, but a baseball bat could be significant to someone else whose loved one played baseball throughout their life. It could be the perfect object, the perfect sign to open the communication between the loved one who has passed and the loved one who remains on the physical plane.

Perhaps someone had a favorite dish, a particular painting they liked or a game they enjoyed playing. All of these can be utilized to create an object or have you become aware of a particular object in your surroundings. That object will strike a thought about a connection to the person who has passed, as only you, the individual, would be able to recognize.

Symbols can be used as a series of communications throughout your daily life. People deal with symbolic objects that can be tapped into to reveal that their loved one was or is around. It is ironic that some of the material things you use on an everyday basis or connect with someone special would actually be used to open up lines of communication after the so-called change known as death. We understand that certain inanimate objects can remind someone of a past love one and that it may not be a connection from our side. It may be because the person is surrounded by their loved one's personal belongings. In this case, it is hard to filter out what was a true sign and what is simply a remembrance due to the proximity and interaction of the person's physical belongings.

However, what we try to do is to have a particular object stand out during a particular time of the day, during a particular event, or something that would make it separate from the rest of the other person's belongings. This would be considered a sign, as that particular object is isolated from the total collection belonging to the past loved one. So, for example, if someone collected coins and the house were full of coins from around the world, what we would do is try to focus in on a particular coin or a particular object.

That item would be singled out in order for you to have a specific sign that your loved one was still around and still in contact. In this case, it could be a coin that was locked in the foot locker, appearing on the loved one's private desk. Perhaps, we might select a stamp from a stamp collector's collection, which is out of its ordinary or organized form.

There are many ways for us to use objects to connect with your side, including the individual objects that are not connected to one's belongings but which simply remind you of the loved one who has passed.

Sometimes, an object does not have to be related to the person at all. It need only remind you of that person. You could have a favorite pastime of watching baseball and your loved one who passed might have had no inclination to follow a particular sport. However, they might send you a sign that has to do with an object you are familiar with. In this example, perhaps phenomena may occur around items related to your pastime. Even though they didn't relate exactly to the loved one who has passed.

At first, you might find it strange and not see the connection, as the loved one had no interest in a particular object; but, if they know that you had interest in that object, then that is what they would present to you in order to gain your attention. We have many different ways to gain your confidence and attention so that we can open lines of communication. Sometimes, they are obvious; other times, they will make you think. If you open your heart and your mind to the possibilities, that makes it much easier for us.

At times, the signs will be quite obvious; so, don't think that you are limited to a few hand-held belongings in order to receive the sign. You can receive them at work, walking in the park, or when you are simply daydreaming. Sometimes the simplest sign is from the simplest object, such as a well-worn sport coat on a stranger walking by. It could be that funny hat that you see lying on the ground or even leaves from a tree as they fall gently and settle on the ground in a certain way that reminds you of past memories you shared with the loved one. These are a few of the many ways of communicating with you through physical objects; and, we hope that you don't limit yourself to certain items, as you might miss that welcoming sign that your loved one has come to say hello and that they are with you for as long as you wish.

The idea behind this chapter is as stated. People need to realize that the objects they are looking for are not the only way to be connected to their loved ones. They see this every day. People expect to see a sign such as a rock falling from the sky and hitting them on the head; but, often, it is the subtle sign that they give to people that goes unchallenged, unaccepted. This is difficult for spirits, as they have worked hard to figure out the proper way of making contact, only to see people pass by with a shrug or skeptical view.

By having people learn these methods of accepting signs, it will increase the amount of communication between our side and yours. People will be relieved to know that their loved ones truly are in contact with them and that they will be able to contact them back. Just look and listen. That should be a lesson for people to learn that the signs are there and it's just a matter of accepting them.

Author's comments:

When senses such as our hearing are not functioning at their top levels, or when we can not distinguish the different aromas in an area, spirits will use objects to gain our attention. This is especially significant when we realize how much importance we place on material things. These objects remind us of past memories and especially past loved ones. It is no surprise then when spirits utilize a special heirloom, a familiar item or any other object while trying to gain our attention.

In the News

I can remember that about one month after my aunt's death, I was reading the Boston Globe on a Sunday afternoon and decided to look at the obituaries. Sometimes they are of famous people; or, perhaps, someone's parent from work or school might be listed. I started to read one on the death of a woman forty-five years old, and I thought how young she was to pass over. Then, I wondered why I was doing this. It was unfortunate, but I didn't know her. I then proceeded to read the next page of news.

Something made me turn the page back to the woman's obituary; but, when I did, I continued to read the obituary but on a different column. It was not about the forty-five-year-old woman. Instead, I was reading about a ninety-five-year-old man. Right there, as I was reading, my aunt's name appeared; because, the man's sister had the same first and last name as my aunt. Also, his mother had the same name as my aunt's mother. I knew that this was not a coincidence but clearly a sign.

Maureen R.

NINE

Dreams

❦

(Channeled from my guides)

*D*reaming is a wonderful way of communicating with your side. It's just so easy for us to tap into your subconscious at this level. We don't need to gain your attention through outside stimulus. You are already open to our hints, whispers, smiles, conversations and waves, as opposed to other methods of contacting you, which we have discussed. Those take a two-way connection. First in the intention for your loved one, in order for you to recognize an object, sound, perhaps a smell or some other similar type of stimulus. With dreaming, we are contacting you through the communication connector. A good example of this might be like a highway that is wide open. As soon as you reach your dream state, the road is open and we can begin.

While you are in the dream state, we can easily communicate with you on different levels. This might sound a little bit complicated; but, it is, in fact, quite simple. We can communicate with you visually, as you can see us and we can see you. Many people can remember their dreams very boldly. We can also connect with you through speech and sound, as we might relive or enjoy a moment together in a world that is as solid as the one you currently exist in.

So it is quite easy for us to contact you through this method, and we have observed that it is quite easy for you to receive us and communicate with us from this method.

You might not always remember the contact that we have had, when you wake up from your dreams; but, sometimes, the contacting communication is so strong that you do remember the meetings you have had with our side. Some of your strongest memorable dreams are actually visitations. You have made it to our side. You may remember that the colors are more vivid, sounds more pronounced, the people you see are recognized and you know instinctively that it is different than one of your ordinary dreams. These are all clues that you have actually tapped in to our side of existence, and you have connected with one of your loved ones.

Dreaming has many parts to it and we will not get too technical for you. It would disturb the momentum of the story, because it can be quite detailed and technical. Actually, thousands of books have been written on dreams and dreaming; and, many of them are very good. However, we are not here to give you the technical schematics of the workings of the dream state but only to emphasize that communication with our side is possible while you are indeed dreaming.

Many times, messages that cannot be conveyed to a loved one through other signs and means will be done through a dream. These messages are a little bit more complex and they sometimes take more energy and effort to get through. This is why we use the method of the dream for this particular communication. It is less taxing on your energy and much less on our side. We feel it is the most efficient way of communicating a message that is a little more complex than just an awareness that your loved one is around.

So some of these messages may contain information concerning your current life; what is happening around you; thoughts concerning family members or friends; or, perhaps, just answering questions that you have been thinking about in recent times.

You should understand that we are sometimes called into your subconscious by thoughts that you have had, and we see this is the proper time to interact with you - in order to help you solve a problem or perhaps to give you information that you're looking for.

And, yes, we use this method in order to contact you and tell you of upcoming events such as the possible passing of a loved one, friend or even that they have arrived safely and are there with their friends now on the other side.

Friends of lost loved ones are also sometimes contacted using this method. It does not have to be a direct family member whom we work through, as sometimes the dream patents are erratic due to health concerns or other variables. So we may come to a friend who happens to be an easier contact and relate messages through them, hoping that this friend will, indeed, transcribe the information for the person for whom it is meant.

I am sure that all of us have, at one time in our lives, been told by a friend or a relative about a dream they had concerning someone who was close to them. I think this is a good example of what they're trying to say right now. It makes a lot of sense that they do come through friends and family, as we are not always able to get these messages ourselves. I guess they try to find the best way to get to us in order to pass on the information.

Yes, this is a correct analysis of the reason why we use other people for communications, as opposed to just going directly to the closest person of the deceased. Some of you have assumed that this communication is only done in the dream stage of deep sleep. It is true that some of our most effective work is completed in this manner. However, we also find that it is easy to tap in to your consciousness while you are daydreaming.

Daydreaming is a wonderful phenomenon that you have at your control. Not only is it a healthy thing for a person to be able to do, but it also gives us the opportunity to touch in, say hello and to give insight and instruction you might sometimes need.

Many times your mind has slipped into a daydream and wandered from thought to thought. This is very similar to being in meditation; thoughts slow down and begin to wander without focusing on any particular thing at any particular point. So this gives us easy access to insert creative ideas, loving memories of past loved ones, problem solving for you and other forms of information that may be needed or wanted at that time.

It is believed that the subconscious can actually be contacted and then used while the conscious state is active. By this, we mean that we can contact you while you're actually concentrating on something else. With daydreaming, it's much easier; because, your focus is at a more random state, as opposed to when you're totally conscious and focused on a particular task at hand. This is when we might use one of our other methods to contact you, such as a sound, smell, or a manipulation of electoral devices, etc.

If you wish to try to remember the content that we have conveyed during your dream state, keep a pen and piece of paper near where you reside. If you wake up in the middle of the night or first thing in the morning or whenever you become conscious and you remember something that's very significant, write it down and you can look back at it after. You will begin to see a pattern of communication with our side. From this, you begin to learn the language of our communication skills.

As for the daydreaming, the same works with it. When you come out of that conscious stream and you have significant information you think might be from our side, write it down and look at it later to see if this information is pertinent to things that are happening in your life or to a loved one who has passed especially if your intentions are there to connect with a loved one. Then, they will use this method to contact you. As we've said before, it can be subtle and very slight; but, the more you realize that the possibility is there, the more that you will pick up the signs and the information will come through.

It does take practice. The more you listen and the more you learn, the better you become at receiving the signs. Don't give up hope and don't despair, as many times the signs will fly right by you; and, you will not be aware of them. This is not entirely your fault. We also may be oblivious to the fact that other stimulus around you is interfering with a message we are trying to send; but, we'll keep trying, if you are open to the experiment of learning the secrets of communication. We called it an experiment, because it's an ongoing interaction between you and us. We try different means, at different times, with different methods in order to see which is most efficient and works the best for each individual.

One last thing about dreams: It's very important for you to understand that we can help you immensely with problems you may be having in your life by just asking us before you slip off into your dream state. If we can and if it's possible, we will help you work out some of the objections or feelings or obstacles that you are facing. We cannot change the future of the actions that you take, for you and only you have control over that. However, we can help you accept the situations that you have entered into and the reasons why you're experiencing the lessons that you are living at that time.

We are here to help you along your way. Please utilize us as often and as much as you wish to learn and grow, as it is our job to help you along your path just as you help us along ours. But first, we must learn the language of communicating with each other's side. Since the beginning of time, dreams have been the most efficient and easiest way for us to communicate with you; so sleep well, train long and enjoy the conversation.

Don't forget to write down your dreams.

Author's comments:

I believe that getting a sign through our dreams is probably one of the most recognized methods available. Many of us have had a dream that we remember as being very vivid and realistic, more so than other dreams. Our loved one may show up in it or perhaps a friend or family member who we recognize. These dreams tend to be remembered a very long time, since they have made a great impression on us and they don't fade, as normal nightly dreams have a tendency to do. Sometimes, such a dream is a contact to say "Hello", while other times it may be sent to give a message or explanation of events or concerns around us. It has become popular for people to keep "dream journals" and I think that is a great idea. If you do have a dream, which you thought was different from one of your ordinary ones, write it down. You might have just have received a sign and you will want to be able to access all the details later on.

A Friend's Message

Authors Comments:

This next story has a few different methods of contact appearing in it, so I thought that it would be a good example to put into this book.

My sister lost a dear friend to cancer this past spring. She had been aware of her friend's illness, but she was not told that it had returned from a previous bout or that the situation was terminal. My sister had suspected that her friend was ill again, but she had not talked to her about it.

Sis began to see her friend in dreams up to one week before her passing. This is not unusual, since, at times, loved ones do try to give notice of their upcoming passage. At times after she passed, she began appearing to me; and, I could see her sitting outside her family's church. She appeared to be happy, giggling and smiling with that mischievous look that we all remembered her having when she was up to no good.

I remember telling my sister that I was getting this visual message. I also described how her friend looked to me, and my sister said that was how she looked when she was younger. I mentioned that her friend was pointing to her black shoes, which were shiny with high heels. She would point to them and then smile and laugh. My sister said that the vision was defiantly her friend, because she always talked about her love of patent leather high heels and that she was unable to wear them for many years. Well, she was wearing them now and looking great!

After giving some more evidential information that only my sister knew, her friend began telling us about our aunt. She said that she was looking out for her and that she was already on their side at times. This is not unusual, because when people begin to get closer to passing, they may slip over and back between the two sides. We see this in late stage Alzheimer's patients and with chronically ill people.

We could not understand this message, because we had just talked to our aunt about coming home from the nursing home, where she had been doing rehabilitation. My sister and I discussed this and came to the conclusion that perhaps our aunt might pass within the next six months or a year.

Within a few days of the message, some medical test results came back regarding our aunt's painful leg, which the doctors had originally diagnosed as sciatica. Well, they were wrong! Not only did she not have sciatica, but the tests showed her to have cancer. It had spread throughout her body and she passed only six days later.

With no warning, we had gone from thinking of bringing her home to planning a funeral. My sister's deceased friend had let us in on the current events in our aunt's life and had given us a heads-up that perhaps she was going to pass very soon. Unfortunately, we didn't accept the full message at that time.

What a wonderful example of a friend's bringing through a message, not only about herself and how happy she was, but also supplying information about our aunt that we didn't know at the time. It was very comforting to realize that the friend was helping one of our love ones, who was in the process of passing. We thank you, S.L.

Joe Higgins

TEN

Angels

❦

(Channeled from my guides)

So, you wish to discuss with us the concept of angels. While we have many who can give you input and insight into this topic, I will help with the translation from the others. So this will be a group effort, and a few will tap in to offer different explanations and how it relates to the subject matter you are writing about.

Angels, for all purposes, guide and look over individuals, groups and constellations, as it may be. Some of us then have more specific roles than others. In my case, I am a guide who is helping you with the written word. My specialty is translating from our side to your side into written text. I've worked with many other writers on your plane and will continue to do this into the future.

However, I do have others who are helping me with the content of the information that is coming through. So it is not my own personal interpretation of these topics, but you're tapping into what is a collective of knowledge attained from a group. This group has been around you your entire life and will continue to be throughout your future development. However, some special angels, or guides, as you might call them, have come into your circle of influence in order for you to explain to the souls on your side how the communication process works.

So your angels that you see in the movies or read about in books come in different sizes and shapes and many have different names and different abilities. This is true to a certain extent; and, at other times, they can be a very simple person or being, who has the ability to shape and secure the best intentions for an individual. By this, we mean simply a guardian angel - someone that is with you throughout your life, and protects you from certain events, but not to interfere with the lessons that you were born here to learn.

They will watch out for you and contact you about future events before you happen upon them. They in no way will interfere with what you have planned and they will not influence you to do something that you have not already agreed to.

They are there to help you along your path, along your journey into learning and developing and enhancing your spiritual agenda. Some are close by you at all times and others are called in for special occasions. These special occasions might have to do with work situations, personal growth development, dealing with others through relationships or even observing and guiding you on one of your traveling experiences.

The angels do, in fact, materialize in your plane in order to contact you when other means are not available or efficient. These angels will take the form of a person who could be a complete stranger but will have a profound effect on your life. They also can take the form of a friend or neighbor, for a very brief time, in order for you to receive a message that is of high importance. These cases are rarer than having interaction with a stranger who may give you information that you need at a particular time.

We see it quite often when people are in distress - and they need to be contacted immediately - that this method is used, as it seems to bring relief and understanding immediately in the case that could be very severe or very high in a person's life.

At times, angels just wish to be around you when you're enjoying your life - and learning and listening - as they can see you grow on your plane and are happy to be part of that experience.

So it's not unusual for someone to experience the love and sharing and guidance of an angel some time throughout their life at a time of turmoil and upheaval. We've been known to work on the battlefields, in the kitchen, while you're driving, or perhaps even when you sleep. All of these particular contact points have been used and many, many others. We ask that you stay open to the possibility of an angel coming into your life, but it is only when it is truly necessary. They will appear and interact with you. Often, it seems at random times; but, do not be surprised if it happens more than once in your life. Just learn from the experience and be happy that you're being watched over and guided and that they're there for your highest and best intentions.

It's quite exciting when angels appear and interact with someone on your side, as results can be quite profound, and the feelings can be of much joy and relief. We have found that the interaction of our angels in your individual lives is something that is of a special nature and that it causes us great enthusiasm that we can work with your side at this level of consciousness. So if something special or extraordinary happens in your life during a time of trouble, don't be surprised if an event or person appears to embrace you with comfort and serenity. Do not push it off as just a coincidence, but it truly is a connection with the divine.

We do not have any favorites concerning different religions or cultures. We work with all those on the physical plane; some are easier to work with than others. Some will not allow us to come through at all; and, therefore, we just are observing their existence throughout their life with no direction or guidance at all, for it has not been requested. If it is not asked for, we cannot intervene on their behalf.

For many others, we are on a constant vigil, to oversee their journey and to bring them hope and serenity and peace throughout their days in the physical plane. This is our main task. When dealing with your side, we realize that some people have many visions of angels in what they can and cannot do. We really don't want to step on anyone's toes and try to clarify exactly which angel or which guide does which particular thing. There are a variety of subjects and intentions that could be associated with angels; but, for the purpose of this book, we wanted you to understand the interaction between us and the individual to a direct sign in communication from the physical plane that we have entered. We hope this clarifies to some extent how we interact with your side and why we do it. It is our intention to try to let you understand that we are always here for you and that we will always be helping, guiding and supporting your efforts throughout your journey, which you call your life.

Author's comments:

The subject of angels has been around since the beginning of time. They are mentioned and referenced in writing from all cultures and religions. One of the things that most of our world can agree upon is that they have been associated with and interacting with the physical plane and, at times, with interceding in our lives.

It is important to remember that angels are open to help guiding and protecting us, and we should keep our hearts open to the possibility that they do exist and can and will interact in our lives.

There have been thousands of books, stories and comments written about these elusive beings, and I am sure that they will continue to fascinate us for many years to come.

Chaos Creates an Angel

My daughter, after being married and living in Florida for a while, had lost a baby; and, soon after, her husband decided to leave her, thus ending her marriage.

What I didn't know, was that down in Florida my daughter had taken to drinking to ease her pain after her husband had left. One day she called and said "Ma, come and get me. I don't have much time left." Now, I'm in Massachusetts going crazy as my daughter is telling me she hasn't much time left. I have a car that probably wouldn't even make it to Florida and no money to get there. Well, the next day an unexpected check came in the mail for three hundred dollars. We still needed a car, as the one we had wouldn't have made it, so we begged and pleaded with everyone we knew to borrow their car.

Someone finally lent us a car and ended up driving down with my husband and me. We got there in 24 hours with me driving almost with closed eyes, because I was so tired. I pull up to this brand new home, which months earlier had this wonderful feeling to it. Yet, the minute I stood near the door, I felt hopelessness all around.

My daughter opened the door and I couldn't believe what I was looking at. This wasn't the daughter who I remembered. She was in such terrible shape that I wanted her to go to the hospital immediately. Her house was almost empty of furniture and it had the worst feeling in it. I told her, "I can't stay in this place. I have to get out." But, we all needed sleep, so we spent the night and were planning n leaving at sunrise in the morning. The next morning, when we all got up, my daughter looked much better; so, we decided to head out and start the long drive back home.

We all decided to take turns driving, as the trip would be about a full day. My daughter volunteered, as she seemed much better after a good night's sleep; so, she took the wheel after me.

We started driving again with her at the wheel. If anyone has been to Florida, you know how fast the traffic can go on the freeways. Well, we are driving down one of highways going with the speed of the traffic about seventy-five miles per hour; and, for a while, it was quite uneventful. I remember sitting there in the front passenger seat saying, "God I am so tired; I need to fall asleep." Well, thank God I never ever fall asleep in a car while I am being driven. All of a sudden, my daughter says to me, "Mom, I'm seeing twinkling colored lights." Before I can react, she passes out behind the wheel of the car going seventy-five.

I went into a quick panic but had enough sense to check to see if her foot was on the gas. It wasn't. So, my head was spinning with thoughts of how can I get out of this without causing a major pile up and a whole lot of dead people. I first decided that I would let the car slow down and pull onto the grass that divided both sides of the highway. Then, I thought if there is a drain or ditch we would be dead. I looked around us and there were wall-to-wall tractor-trailers and cars surrounding our vehicle. Now, I am still steering the car saying, "God, show me what to do."

The next thing was the biggest miracle I know I will see in my lifetime. Well, God heard me loud and clear. He made an opening where I just turned the wheel and was able to drive across all the lanes and end up on the other side on the grass.

I wish with all my heart that everyone could have seen this. It was like some people were told to speed up and the others told to slow down. It was a perfectly angled path going across the highway that let us cross all the lanes and safely stop the car. I got the car stopped, the engine shut off and I raced over to my daughter, who was still unconscious. I couldn't feel a pulse, and I was trying to open her mouth in case she was biting her tongue from a possible seizure. Now, I'm in a big state of panic. Do I call the cops first or do CPR? I needed both. What I didn't know, people had seen what happened while I was crossing the highway and called an ambulance and the police. As I brought the car to a halt, I noticed that this tractor-trailer had pulled over and a man was walking toward me. He asked if she was alright and I said I didn't think so. Now, I must admit that, when I saw the truck and the driver, that something was different about this man. Well, he went over to my daughter – who is still unconscious – and touches the side of her neck, turns to me and says she will be fine. Just the way he turned and the knowing in his voice told me this wasn't an ordinary person.

He started to walk away; and, as I watched him, something kept saying, "There is something different about him. He isn't a real person." Finally, I started running to catch up to him to stop him, so I could thank him. I grabbed his arm and said, "Thank you." When I did, it felt like nothing I had ever touched. This man was no normal man. I just knew I had met a real, live angel. I knew in my heart whatever he did to my daughter saved her life; everything was alright.

I then ran back to my daughter, who was being treated by paramedics and was now awake. As I turned back to look at the stranger and his truck, it was gone. How it could have left in that gridlock of traffic in less than a minute, I'll never know.

Everyone at the scene agreed with me that something intervened and saved many lives that day. Even the state trooper said there was no way I could have done what I had done with the car and crossing the highway without help from God.

To this day, I can still feel the touch of that angel.

Patti C.

ELEVEN

When and Where Do They Do It?

❦

(Channeled from my guides)

*W*e would like to talk to you about how we communicate with you at different times of the day and at different levels. We can communicate with you while you are actually doing your daily activities. We do not wish to interfere with your daily activities. We only desire to let you know that we are around to assist you and guide you. Whenever the need arises, we can do this through subtle signs, such as a light touch or a breeze across your face. We can even use a sign or symbol - for just a split second - to halt your thoughts and have you think of us. This is our way of letting you know that we around you and willing to help you in any manner that you may need us. Other times, we will make a valiant effort to secure your attention by alternate means. In this manner, we are realizing that your attention might not be able to be attained, so we step back, wait and listen till you are ready to accept messages and communications.

Actually, the best time to contact you is when your mind is at ease and your body is relaxed. Seeing that the largest obstacle with the communicating method is interference from outside sources, we try to pick a time when there is the least amount of outside stimulus grabbing your attention. This can mean overall activity surrounding you, or even things that are on your mind and have kept you occupied throughout the day. So, you could be in a crowded ballpark or home alone with your mind filled with worries and responsibilities and this would delay any sign we wish to come through with.

However, if your mind is at ease and your body is relaxed and you are not focused on some particular situation that is going on at a particular time; then, we might try to come through and contact you - even if you are in a crowded ballpark, or alone at home. It might be sometime while you are driving in your car and your mind begins to wander off. It could be when you are thinking of some event, some experience that you might have had with your loved one to bring that person into your consciousness. We also have the ability to use the electronic phenomena in your vehicles, as we may manipulate your listening devices such as a CD or radio. We can use other means of contacting you in a vehicle such as sounds with specific music, smells and visual signs, too.

So the timing of the communication depends on the individual and the current state that the individual is in, such as how open they are to receiving a message and how open they are to the possibility of contact from a deceased loved one. These are important questions that would have to be answered first before an attempt would be made.

Sometimes, it is difficult for us to determine the exact time that we want to make the attempt to contact you. However, with the right probing and investigation into the life of the individual we are trying to contact, we can find the perfect time when we might be able to slip in and give you that so important sign that your loved one is actually in contact with you. Now, some of this might be in the middle of the day, while they are sitting in a classroom gazing out a window. For others, it might be while they are driving to and from work, as their mind wanders off. Perhaps, that time is just before someone awakes from a sound sleep. That is always a prime time for us to try to make a connection; and, of course, we try during your dream state. This is often an effective time for us to slip in and try to make contact.

On your side, time is very rigid and strict, as you have schedules and responsibilities during the day. You usually sleep at certain hours in your day and have other activities to attend to, depending on your daily time allowance. However, when we decide to try to connect with you, we look more at how you are feeling. How your body is reacting to outside influences upon you will affect the health of your mind and spirit. This is very important to the process. So time to us is not the same as time you would use when you run your day.

We do see excellent results while people are sleeping, as we have mentioned to you about connecting through dreams. This falls into the category of one's mind at ease and the body being relaxed. Also, we find that when you are approaching waking up from a sound sleep or, perhaps, a daytime nap, this, too, is also a good time to connect with you. This is due to many of your burdens, worries and random thoughts being pushed to the side, making it easier for a sign, a contact, to come through.

While you are beginning to awaken from a sound sleep, we can put bits of information into your subconscious that will soon come into your consciousness as you begin your day. These may be followed by more evidential signs throughout the day, as these could be used as a prelude to upcoming events of contact.

For some people, we like to use the sounds of nature, as they often bring back many fond memories of past loved ones and can be relaxing at the same time. The sounds of the wind blowing through the trees, raindrops hitting the ground or the ocean crashing on a beach are effective. All are very good, natural sounds that we will use to get your attention. If one is in the natural environment where the sounds are produced, not only will it bring relaxation and calmness, but it also settles the mind for us to bring in certain thoughts. These thoughts will constitute the beginning of the sign.

So you don't have to be in a specific place at a specific time in order to receive a sign. However, in certain areas or certain locations, a sign can be more easily presented to someone than at other times or places. If you are very busy at work trying to do five things at once, this would not be a good time to give you a sign, as it surely would just blend into the background and would not gain your attention. If you are driving in heavy traffic and you must focus on the road or the weather conditions that are around you, we would not even attempt to give you a sign at that time, for we would not want to distract you. Our intention is not to take away your daily living activities but to find a way to meld into them in order to make that connection.

At other times, when it is necessary to contact you, due to the importance of the message, we **will** make an overt sign to you to grab your attention if your are busy with your everyday matters. This can be used - not only if you are busy at work or with your daily responsibilities – but, also, if your emotions are distracted and distorted. In this case, we may use a more vibrant sign to contact you, thus enabling us to grab your attention in the midst of your distractions.

There are certain times and places that are more advantageous to receiving a sign. So you are not limited by location. It is more about how you are feeling in your mental and physical state that will determine when and where we will come to you.

At times, after one has lost someone close to them, a person can become so grief stricken that the environment for the connection to come through is blocked. When this happens, we will look for other avenues to send a message, a sign, to let you know that your loved one is in contact with you. This can be done through communicating information to a friend or family member. As the body stabilizes in its emotional and physical state, we then can try to connect directly with the person.

The best piece of advice we can give you is to be in the proper mind and the proper environment to receive a quality sign from your loved one. And although we say "environment," we don't necessarily mean a particular place. We mean your overall emotional and physical state.

So stay open to the possibilities of communicating with our side. Keep yourself as healthy as possible. Smiling and laughter are wonderful cleansers of the human spirit; and, they can open a pathway to the communication between you and your loved one, who has passed.

The Wig

A good example of how a loved one can come through a friend or family member in order to pass on a message is related in the following incident that happened to me.

One evening, while I was preparing to meditate, I encountered a personality coming into my thoughts; and, as a medium, I identified it as someone who wanted to come through and pass along some information. I immediately recognized who the person was, because I had met this woman the year before. Jane was the aunt of a close friend of mine and had passed about six months prior to this event.

Since I was trying to be very disciplined with my meditation training, I accepted her into my consciousness, I said hello and welcomed her. I told her that I would be able to connect with her at another time but that I was in the midst of meditating and training myself and that I did not want to be disturbed. When you are a medium, you have to set guide lines as to when anyone can come through or your mind will be cluttered with conversational thoughts all day long. However, if someone comes through who I immediately recognize out of the blue, then it usually means something very important and I need to pay attention.

She was persistent, just as she had been in her life on our physical plane. Therefore, I stopped my meditation, and then allowed Jane to come through with the information that needed to be passed on to her niece.

She immediately told me that she was doing fine, that she was no longer in pain and she was smiling broadly and moving about. Now, the strange part: As she was telling me that she was in good spirits, no pun intended, she reached up to her head and removed a wig. She began to remove the wig and then place it back on her head. She did this repeatedly. Then, she removed the wig and shook it in her right hand, while smiling broadly and laughing out loud. Next, she grasped the wig and held it with two hands to her heart and placed it back on her head.

Jane then mentioned that she did not want to keep me from my scheduled meditation, but she only wanted to come through so I could pass the message along that she was happy and healthy and to say "hi" to her niece. When I asked her about the wig, she just looked at me and smiled with the widest grin imaginable; but, she did not comment.

At that point, I wished her much love and peace, I thanked her for coming and told her that I would convey the message to her family. Then, her energy pulled away, and I continued with my meditation.

After my meditation, the force of the message that had been brought through to me was so strong that I felt as though I needed to connect with the family to let them know that their aunt had come to me, telling me that she was fine and no longer in pain.

I immediately went to my computer and started to compose an e-mail message. I had not spoken to or been in any contact with her family in over three months. As I prepared the e-mail message, Jane's face kept appearing in my mind as being happy, joyful and actually laughing. As a result, I was looking forward to passing on this message to her family. I completed the e-mail message and sent it off to her niece.

I closed out of my computer and turned it off for the evening. In less than ten minutes, my phone began to ring; and, I had a strange sensation that it had something to do with the e-mail I had just sent.

When I answered the phone, I recognized the voice immediately. It was Jane's niece. She was happy to hear from me, since it had been a long time since we had chatted. She said that she just received the e-mail message and had to call me right away because of the events that had occurred at her house that same afternoon.

It seems that Jane's husband, who lived next door, had been in quite an emotional state while talking to the niece and her other aunt. He was looking for a specific wig that his wife used to wear when she went out in public, because he wanted to give it to his new girlfriend. When I say new girlfriend", I am being kind; because, as I found out, he was quite friendly with her before his wife had passed. As he stood in the niece's living room demanding to know where Jane's wig was stored, the niece and the other aunt were astonished at his request.

They just couldn't believe that he was so petty and thoughtless as to demand a wig that had been used by his wife while she was battling cancer, just so that it could be given to this other woman. Throughout that afternoon, they looked through the two houses in every closet, every box, and everywhere imaginable for the wig that was so coveted by the husband of the deceased.

When the niece told me this story, I found it very curious that the message had come through that evening concerning events that happened during that same afternoon. She could not believe how strange it was and I couldn't understand the meaning of the message until the niece explained to me what happened next.

After thoroughly searching both homes and not finding a clue to the whereabouts of the wig, the niece came up with an idea and picked up the phone. She thought that there might be a slight chance that someone else would know the location of this so valued wig. An older gentleman answered the phone, remembered meeting the niece and, of course meeting Jane. He remembered these details, because Jane had only recently passed away and he was of the owner of the funeral home. When the niece asked if perhaps the wig was stored somewhere at the home, the owner explained exactly where the wig was located. It seems that while setting up and organizing her own funeral, Jane have requested that one particular wig be buried with her, since it had brought her so much comfort and peace during the last few months of her life.

Now, it all came together. Now, I understood why Jane had come through that evening to show me that she actually had the wig with her, and it was not going to get into the hands of her husband's lover. That is why she was dancing joyfully and holding the wig close to her heart. She knew that she had gotten the last laugh!

Jane's niece and sister were so overjoyed with the message that had come through that they laughed and cried, knowing that their loved one had truly come through with an appropriate message for that exact situation at just the right time.

This is a perfect example of when a loved one needs to come through with a specific message at a specific time and cannot get through directly to his/her loved ones. At such a time, they may come through to a friend.

In order to try to get that message through, Jane probably tried to get through directly to the niece but was not successful. Therefore, going through me, a medium, was the perfect second choice. She knew I would relate the message as soon as I received it and she was correct. If a love one needs to come through, they will find a way, just be open to any possibilities.

Joe Higgins

One Ringie Dingie, Two Ringie Dingie

During the next few days after my aunt had passed, late at night, I began to hear the house phone ringing downstairs while I was upstairs. The problem was that it was not ringing on any of the phones upstairs, not even on the phone next to my bed. This situation should not have been possible, but it happened on at least three or four different occasions.

Then, in a dream a few days later, my cell phone was ringing with that unique tune it has and I thought, "Who is trying to contact me?" I soon realized who it must be; because this would be a perfect sign, since I work for the telephone company and my aunt had worked for the phone company for forty-three years.

Maureen R.

Part Three
How Do I Do It?

TWELVE
How Do I Do It?

❦

(Channeled from my guides)

*J*t all starts with concentration on your part. You have to be willing and able to silence your mind in order for us to communicate with you, and this is easier for some people to do than for others. We recommend sitting in a dark room with little or no light and putting on some soft music. This will enable you to slow your thoughts down and to relax without lots of stimulus affecting your brain. It may take some time and practice; but slowly, you will learn to quiet your mind and random thoughts that you have constantly running through your head will slow down and begin to evaporate.

At times, it will be more difficult for some people than for others. You all have daily activities that are constantly running through your mind, such as your soccer practice, picking up groceries, delivering children to different places, running errands and living your daily lives. All this action creates thoughts and patterns in your brain. You think about them throughout the day, consciously and subconsciously. When it comes time to relax and meditate, these thoughts are still popping into your head. You are asking questions of yourself. Did I forget to do something? Did I do the right thing in that situation? Did I do something wrong? What am I going to do tomorrow? How do I feel? Why do I feel like that? Why do others feel like that? Did I make someone happy today? Did I make someone sad? Am I worrying too much? Am I able to accomplish everything that I wanted to do today?

These are a few of the things that will run through your mind when you sit quietly in a darkened room trying to communicate with us. These are also the things that you have to learn to push out of your mind before we are able to effectively communicate with you. It is possible for these things to occupy your mind throughout your entire life, to the point where you'll never be in communication with your loved ones who have passed. As you will see in other parts of this book, they will try to communicate with you; but, for you, that communication will be limited by the activities that you have sent to your brain concerning your daily living habits. At times, you allow yourself to slow down and relax. Some of you call this "vacation", while others call it "a timeout."

We would prefer to call this state of relaxation "a time to slow down and smell the roses." We mean that you'll actually take time out of the day to sit, meditate and relax to quite your thoughts. This will give us time to learn the pattern of your life in order to find the best possible time to communicate with you. We have seen that it is easiest to communicate telepathically; while, at other times, it is just as easy to communicate with sounds, smells, touch, and other avenues.

We do like to let you know that the easiest way to communicate with us is by opening your heart and allowing us to come through that loving portal into your consciences. At such times, you are allowing us to have permission to contact you. It opens the door for the beginning of the communication lesson. Now, to gain a level of communication one would feel comfortable with in order to communicate with our side, it is just a matter of practice, perseverance and willingness.

To make the connection, sometimes it takes a minute amount of effort; and, at other times, it is easier to move a mountain with a thumbnail. However, everyone has the ability to communicate with us; and, when I say "us," I mean your guides, your loved ones and the higher realms of consciousness. We see that some people have a special connection from a very young age, while others take a lifetime to become accustomed to our thoughts. It is not uncommon for a child to be in direct communication with us while they are playing, while they are learning to live in the environment of their existence.

As you grow and accumulate more experiences, your mind becomes accustomed to learning, analyzing and understanding the events and actions of your existence on the material plane. This begins to build up a barrier between your existence and our plane. However, it can be penetrated and dissolved as easily as a speck of flour in a gallon of water. Yet, at other times, this barrier can solidify as hard as cement.

We hope that the lessons people learn from this book will help them open up their hearts and begin to learn the wonderful life of communicating with the other side, our side. We see it as combining your divine being with your home, where you came from, your eternal connection to God.

We've just touched upon some of the ways that you can communicate with us, and we will give you more details as we go along. But, for now, we would like to keep it as simple as possible. Your ability to communicate is unlimited. However, the obstacles you can put in the way are also unlimited. It is you who must decide if you wish to open that door and learn to access the bridge that has always been there.

Author's comments:

We might think that the whole process of "how I can connect" is limited to just a few chosen individuals, that it is some complex, mystical, ancient possibility. It is not that way at all; we all have the ability to do it ourselves.

The thing to remember is that giving permission is the first step in allowing any type of contact. You are allowing yourself the honor of practicing what is a normal phenomenon to our natural spiritual being. It is part of our make up.

It was interesting when they mentioned, "and, when I say "us," I mean your guides, your loved ones and the higher realms of consciousness." This is important, since you are not limited to just contacting a particular person, but to your guides for learning and support throughout your life.

We are not ever alone. Ask for help. It is there for you. I do!

THIRTEEN
How to Connect to Us

❦

(Channeled from my guides)

So you wish to learn how to connect to us?

*A*ctually, there are many different methods you may use to enable the link up to our existence and to communicate with us at will. Several of these means have been described in this book plus how we initiate the contact with you. What we would like to talk about at this time is how you can initiate the contact with us.

In order to begin the process of trying to communicate with us, you should be in a very comfortable position. By this, we mean physically. But, just because you might be relaxed and sitting comfortably, it does not necessarily mean that you're prepared to open up and connect to us. There are many different dynamics available to open the communication between us. Some are easy and can be done at will, while others take years to master and to develop into a spirit communicator, which you might call a medium.

Children are natural-born communicators because they have not been overburdened by outside stimulus and responsibilities of your real world. To them, everything is interesting and a new learning experience. So they can put their whole selves into learning something new, as opposed to adults with other responsibilities in the back of their minds, which, at times, can hold them back in the development and attempt to communicate with us.

The methods that you can use to contact us are by simple thought. All it takes is just a simple thought about one of your love ones and you have opened up the communication channel. On our side of existence, we can feel your emotions, your thoughts, your prayers. It is much easier for us to get your sign than it is for you to receive a sign from us.

Prayer is often associated with a religious connection. In many cases, this is true, but it is also a basic form of communicating your thoughts or your voice to our side. As many people have been trained on how to pray from an early age, they already have the groundwork for communicating with us at any time they desire. You see, a labyrinth of connection schemes is not necessary in order for you to make your thoughts and ideas known to us. Simply learning to be open to receive back some of your questions is what needs to be finely tuned.

So there were a few things you can do as an adult in order to facilitate trying to connect to us. One of these is asking us to receive your signs and communications. This will give us the permission to engage with you and communicate with you at our discretion. If someone does not wish to communicate with our side, we have no authority to try to contact that person. It has been done; and, at times, it does happen, but this is not the normal, everyday routine, as you would put it. You do have total control over how the communication will be viewed. So prayer is the main means of communicating with us and this can be done any time and from any place.

Studying and learning the practice of meditation is another form of communication with our side, if you wish to bring it to that level. You can learn to quiet your mind, to relax your body and to ask for a sign or signs for us to communicate with you; and, this will open the door to your learning how to contact and connect with us. This method of relaxation is also very beneficial to the human body as well as to the spirit. We say *the spirit*, because, when the human body is relaxed and not concerned with outside stimuli, it is focusing on learning. At such times, the spirit grows through learning and lessons that have been created for it to discover and explore.

If you wish to connect to us, your setting a specific time, specific day or specific routine would work well. It's like going to a classroom at a certain time to learn a new lesson. We will be there for you if you decide to do some learning every day at a particular time, every other day or whatever your schedule allows. Remember, the more you do a thing, the better you become at it. For others, brief contact is all that is requested; and, this is all that we can request to happen. You see, it may be enough for individuals to realize that their spiritual beings are not limited to the physical world and that they are in tune to the whole, the Divine, which they have come from.

Authors Comments:

I believe that there are various ways for us to connect to our guides, loved ones and higher realms - such as through one's dreams, thoughts or intentions. Learning certain relaxing habits could enhance the probability of a successful connection.

Keeping your physical body in good shape, eating properly and getting enough sound sleep are good, basic ideas to start with.

Learning meditation and practicing it regularly would be a strong foundation for the learning process.

*Also, it is important to remember always to do this from your heart. Asking for loving guidance and support for your **highest and best intentions** will enable you to be sure that the contact which you seek, and the information you receive, is from a higher, compassionate source.*

Before I start any contact, I always say a little prayer and remember to thank those who have helped and guided me. I start and end my day with thanks and gratitude for all the learning opportunities that have come my way and for all the support I have received and will receive from the higher realms.

FOURTEEN

How to Look and Listen for Signs

❦

(Channeled from my guides)

*J*t seems you all have a tendency to be very protective about your space and any energy around it. This seems to be the first hurdle that must be passed in order to make contact with our side. It is because you are truly a spiritual being that you are quite aware of your surroundings and how you feel in certain situations.

You all have had experiences, such as knowing when someone is standing behind you or, perhaps, you feel uneasy about entering a certain location. You might not have any proof to base this feeling on, as it's just a gut feeling. This is the sense that you are tapping into, this part of your divine makeup, which helps with communications.

So the first thing to learn is how to let down this protective field that you have around you and to begin to look and listen for the signs that you have asked for. When we mentioned *a protective field*, we meant this in the sense that it is used on your physical plane - to give you extra information concerning your environment. In the past, it was used, to a higher degree, in order for survival. Today, it might be used to tap into in order to make specific decisions or when seeking guidance.

Another main theme of this chapter is to let go of the everyday worries and responsibilities that seem to occupy your mind at all times. It is difficult to look or listen for signs from us when you are preoccupied by the activities of your daily living.

So another example of letting your guard down is to put aside all the thoughts and questions that your mind tries to process in what seems like every minute of the day. As we have mentioned before, pursuing techniques such as meditation will help you to relax your mind and to let your guard down so that contact can be made.

Once you have practiced and mastered the ability to relax your mind and body at will, the signs that you seek will come to your attention much more easily than before. We are not asking that you be on a constant vigil for signs, such as sounds and smells, but only by putting your body and mind in a certain well-controlled presence will you be able to pick up the subtle differences in the energy that is around you. This will make it much easier for us to tap into, to place a thought, a physical object, or to create the sign that you have been looking for.

After loved ones have passed, they often wish to send a sign to their loved ones on the physical plane that they are truly still in existence and can connect to them. There can be much activity in trying to send a sign of contact during this time; but, as in the case of someone who is not looking or listening for a sign, it goes unseen, unfelt, and undiscovered.

So with some basic training and studying on how to relax your mind and your body, and by giving permission to us, you put yourself into a position of being able to accept connections from your loved ones on our side.

If you are unsure or you are easy about opening up, looking and listening for our signs, just remember that simply giving permission for a sign to come through will enable it to be available.

Authors Comments:

It sounds like good advice when they mention," to let go of the everyday worries and responsibilities that seem to occupy your mind at all times." We all have a tendency to fill our minds with everyday worries, expectations and lists of things to do. How are we supposed to recognize a sign when there is no room left in our active consciousness?

By letting some of the everyday thoughts, that seem to constantly via for our attention, go by and releasing the extra baggage of worry we will open up more opportunities for our conscience mind to access the signs that are being sent our way.

Take time out of your day to just soak in the reality of your existence. This will clear your mind, readjust your focus and allow any sign the ability to be successfully received.

Time to Do Your Hair

One of the first encounters with contact from the other side was in the very early morning of my mother's funeral. My family and I had been at the wake the night before; and, after it was over, we all ended up leaving together and going to a relative's house for refreshment and a light meal.

The day had been long and we had the funeral to attend to in the morning, so I decided I should get home, because it was about ten o'clock p.m. I arrived home shortly there after, put my things away and headed straight upstairs to bed. I went out like a light since it had been a highly emotional day and I was quite tired, I ell asleep immediately. At about three o'clock a.m., I awoke to a load noise coming from the bathroom. I got out of bed and could not believe what I was hearing. The blow-dryer in the bathroom was on full blast! I walked in and shut it off, thinking how could this be happening and then I returned to bed.

The next day, I was very surprised that I was not frightened or kept awake by that event. Instead, I had been very calm and peaceful and I did go right back to sleep as though nothing happened. It was then that I realized my mother had sent me a sign that she was OK. and just wanted to say hello.

Maureen R.

FIFTEEN
How to Ask for a Sign

❦

(Channeled from my guides)

The first thing we need to start with is your giving us permission to contact you and to send you a sign. Often, this permission is not an outright saying, such as, "It's okay to contact me." Instead, you can give us permission by the thoughts and emotions that you are thinking and feeling. If a loved one has recently passed and you're thinking about them and wish they were around; then, that in itself is a form of asking for a sign and giving permission.

At other times, you can come out directly and say, "Please send me a sign." So, through the various ways of asking for a sign - either directly or through your thoughts or emotions -we can realize that you want to be contacted. Our side determines what is the best time and place for the connection to occur.

If you do ask for a sign, do not put any limitations on the manner in which we may send it to you. We have found that we have the better intuition as to when a sign would be accepted successfully. That means, if you are off on a fishing trip and you want to get a sign from your dad or grandfather, and that the sign you're looking for is to be catching a big fish, don't be disappointed if you come home empty-handed. For we might find it easier to communicate that sign later on that evening or, perhaps, within the next couple of days.

So do not put boundaries or restrictions on your requests to receive a sign, as this limitation will only increase the odds of not having a successful contact with our side.

If you ask for a sign with an open heart and it is for your highest and best intentions, then the chances of your receiving a sign will be heightened.

Sometimes, we see people expecting a certain sign; and, when they don't receive it, they get very anxious and confused. It is not our intention for this to occur. But, most often, it is because of the person's expectations. Those expectations have set them up for this emotional turmoil to occur. Set your intention and let it go. If the possibility of connecting with our side is to happen, then it will. If there is a particular reason why a sign would not be given; and, there are many reasons, then they will not be disappointed, as the expectations have not been to the highest degree.

Your asking for a sign will put certain energies into motion that, hopefully, will cumulate in your receiving and accepting of the sign we provide.

Is it possible to ask for a sign for someone else? Yes, you can request that a sign be given to another individual from a deceased love one. As long as the individual is willing to accept the sign and it will not be emotionally disturbing to them, then every effort will be taken to accept your request.

An example might be a parent, who wishes to have a sign for their daughter or son from one of their favorite grandparents that may have passed. In this case, everything possible would be done to make that request available to the child. However, if someone specifically requests that no contact be made, we also must abide by that request. Some people do not wish to contact a past relative due to a possible conflict with that person when both were on the physical plane. We understand this, and we are obligated not to interfere with your lives, as you are learning the lessons that your soul has come to that plane to be taught.

If you don't want any contact with someone; but, you talk to the deceased person or emotionally invite them in, then they would become confused and try to contact you.

As we mentioned elsewhere in the book, if a sign is requested, it is important to remember that you need to be in a stable emotional state so that a sign will be available to come through. This just makes it easier on our part, although we can make contact even under very trying times that the living individual may be going through. If they are confused or emotionally unstable, then we will limit any contact that we would have with them, even if you requested it. We would not want to upset the balance of anyone's physical and emotional health.

Author's comments:

Asking for a sign seems to be about intention. If one is truly interested in contact, then we only need to have an intention for the process to begin. What we learn in this guided message is that we should not put boundaries on our request. Do not limit the opportunities for them to make contact, because they seem to know the process better than we do.

SIXTEEN

How to Understand and Accept a Sign

❧

(Channeled from my guides)

*A*ccepting a sign can be very simple for some people; and, to others, it can create a complex maze of emotional and physical turmoil. What we mean by this is that someone might say, "Oh I just received a sign from Uncle John." Others may become confused and think that something out of the ordinary just happened but that it might not be an actual connection from their uncle. To accept a sign, first you must be in the right emotional and physical state to be aware that an actual sign has been presented to you.

One of the main ingredients is your willingness and openness to receiving a sign. This is simple in its explanation, but, at times, it is difficult to practice. Just be open to the possibility, remember to say "thank you" when you realize that communication has been made, and we will know that you truly have accepted this invitation to communicate.

To understand the sign that we give you, one must first understand the process of how we go about making that connection. We have explained some of this process earlier in this book. However, we would like to add that we have the ability to know when a particular sign has a chance to be understood and, therefore, a chance at being successful in communicating with a loved one. There are times that we will give a sign; but, for various reasons, the recipient will not understand or will become confused and the attempted connection will lead to a failure.

In the signs that we give you, we try to relate to specific information and common themes that are associated with a loved one who has passed. For example, we would not try to give you a sign from a specific person using a particular object or sound that would be totally alien to the deceased's personality or history. Common associations, humorous experiences and individual peculiarities are focused upon. When determining the type of sign that will be given to you, we try to make it as easy, simple and effortless as possible for you to accept and understand the sign and from whom it has come.

We do have a request for all of you. Do not repeatedly ask for signs after receiving many when you are not willing to accept any of them. It takes much time and energy to make a connection, and it can be very tiring to see all our hard work go for naught, due to your unwillingness to accept the sign that you have already seen and understood. We understand that you have doubts and confusion about signs, in general, and we take this into consideration when organizing our efforts at connecting with you. However, at some point, individuals who are unwilling to accept a sign that they *know* to be authentic will not be given any more contact. We have seen this many times and it is so discouraging to those who have worked so hard on our side that we can not continue with the effort.

Author's comments:

I have actually seen this in person from a woman who attended a local charitable fair while I was donating mediumistic readings. She came to me about two family members who had passed and I mentioned that they had been trying to send her signs that they were around her. She finally admitted to me that, yes she had seen the signs, but she still doubted them. She kept asking for more signs without accepting any of the others. Her relatives informed me that they would send one more sign to her; and, if she did not accept it, there would be no more. They told me it would be large and obvious. One month later, when I ran into the woman, she smiled and told me they had come through and that, this time, she finally accepted the sign.

I was happy for her and asked how they did it. She said that she had been thinking of her father as she pulled up to an intersection on a busy road and wondering if she would be given the opportunity again to witness a sign from him and to be able to say "yes" and thank him for it. As the light turned green and before she could pull out, a tractor trailer passed through the intersection. She began to cry as she noticed that the advertisement on the side of that huge truck had the same childhood nick name her father used to call her throughout her life.

Two Months Later

Today, I was reading one of my aunt's pocket calendars, as she kept detailed notes of her ongoing schedules through out most of her life. Some might call them journals; but, for someone who had a busy work schedule all her life, the daily pocket planners were the way to go.

Looking at some of her final months was interesting; because she tried to keep a schedule, even though her physical body was starting to give out. "Today I went to Stop and Shop; in the afternoon, called a friend". As she started to feel more run down and the weather became colder and more unpredictable, many of the notations would show her staying in most of the day.

Frequently, it would say "doctor appointment in morning", "stayed in the balance of the day". "Had my hair done", "Stayed in the balance of the day". "Went food shopping in morning but returned due to weather, stayed in the balance of the day".

I found that expression odd, since I have never heard of any expression like that in my 50 years. So, whether she went to the market or the doctor's, she would very often end her entry "stayed in balance of the day".

That night, before I went to bed, I said, "Gee, you have not contacted Joe or me in a while, I wonder why.

The very next morning, as I was driving to work, I began to think about her notes in her daily calendar; and, within two minutes, as the weather man on the radio was wrapping up his report, he said that it would be partly cloudy and humid for "the balance of the day".

I began to smile and a warm feeling come over me, knowing that I had received another sign from my loving aunt.

Maureen R.

SEVENTEEN

The Difference between Wanting and Getting an Authentic Sign

❧

(Channeled from my guides)

The difference between wanting and getting an authentic sign is rooted in the recipient's intentions and willingness to accept the possibility that no sign will be given. For various reasons, not all requests for signs from a loved one are fulfilled. The reason is that many people would be willing to accept a sign from their loved one, who has passed, but are not able to accept it due to certain religious, cultural or community guidelines.

At times, these situations can be worked out and signs can be brought through. But at other times, we do not wish to create upsetting circumstances by having individuals search their consciousness about being allowed to accept a sign from the other side. Under no circumstance, do we wish to bring any harm, additional suffering or confusion to the person who has lost a loved one. If we suspect that an individual might have a difficult time in dealing with a sign that they might receive, then that sign will not be initiated.

For our attention is to bring relief, hope, understanding and love. Anything that might be upsetting or cause one to challenge their belief systems to the extent that it might possibly cause them grief or harm would not be allowed through.

Some people may unwillingly associate certain phenomena to a sign from a past loved one. There will be an overwhelming willingness to accept any and all possibilities with the joy coming from the search and the adventure of it all instead of the actual receiving of an authentic sign.

Others also may associate unrelated circumstances to someone who has passed on. In these cases, it is not our intention that these associations be based on true authenticity. Some people have a tendency to see what they wish to see and to believe anything that appears even remotely connected to their loved one. In such a case, when an authentic sign is actually given and the person receives it and accepts it, it loses some of its intention and power, as it has been thrown in with many random events and thus loses its potency to bring joy and intense love.

If one assumes that a sign has been received and they have doubts about its authenticity, we can help them discover if this is a true connection with a spirit. An authentic sign, whether subtle or obvious, will have distinct energies surrounding it. Awareness will register much more strongly with the authentic sign. Even if a person might have a problem with accepting a particular sign, the connection that one will make between the past loved one and the sign will be quite evident. This is why many times people are stopped in their tracks. It happens, as the awareness is so strong. Feelings associated with a sign are also very important to proving its authenticity. If the sign is recognized and feelings are stirred, the chances that the sign actually has come from their loved one are very high. If there is a strong sense of love, sadness, laughter or joy, then these, too, are proof that an authentic piece of communication has been brought into their consciousness.

Many times, people will want to receive an immediate sign only to lose their patience, causing themselves more grief and unhappiness. This may disrupt the communication methods we try to use, as they have altered their emotional state to the point that authenticity might not be able to be confirmed. If one's intentions are still positive and their ability to accept a sign is still stable, then other attempts will be made.

Many times, a message will be repeated in a short time frame from an original one. Even if the first sign is understood and accepted, a second message can be sent to reinforce any doubt that may remain in your conscious or unconscious mind. Frequently, we will hear a response such as, "Okay, okay I got it!" This gives us great comfort, as not only have you accepted the sign, but your belief in it is without doubt. Other times, a second message will be given, as the first sign may have awakened you to the possibility of communication with a loved one, but you are unable to comprehend the full meaning of this first contact.

We do not wish for you to dwell on trying to distinguish between an authentic sign in your own consciousness and wishing one to be true, as this will only cause unnecessary anxiety. If you are open and accepting to the possibilities that an authentic sign will come to you, then there is no need to put your consciousness in turmoil by trying to differentiate between multiple signs.

Sometimes, if you think it is a sign, that is all that is needed. For your thinking about your deceased loved one or friend would be enough to open the loving connection between our world and yours. We would not even have to initiate a sign for a connection to be made. For if you truly believe that you have received the sign from your departed, then the link has been made and you can enjoy the loving and comforting emotions that are associated with it.

We have seen some obvious signs come into doubt, as people receiving them cannot believe how blatant and obvious a sign truly can be. Some people think if it's too good to be true, it just can't be true. Unfortunately for them, this is another missed opportunity for that special connection.

There is an expression people on your side sometimes like to use: If it looks like a duck, walks like a duck and quacks like a duck, it's a duck. So, if you are driving down the highway someday and you are thinking of that special person who has passed over and a car or truck passes you by and that special person's name appears on the license plate or truck advertisement, then you should realize that you have just gotten a sign from your loved one. For it's not that we have manipulated a license, or advertisement, but we have put your loved one's thought into your consciousness before the visual sign comes into focus.

There are many different ways for us to gain your attention some big, some small, and even some that you would not even understand but would, in the long run, give you comfort and relief from the loss of that special person in your life.

Author's Comments:

Separating a want from getting an authentic sign starts with the individual's intentions. If you are focusing on the search for a sign and are willing to accept any and all possibilities, the chance that you will be able to differentiate a real one from general every day stimulus is small. The guides also talked about the stronger emotional connection to an authentic event. Using your gut feelings is probably the best way to judge if you have received the actual sign.

If I experience a chill when observing a possible sign, then I definitely know I have been contacted. If a sign comes out of nowhere and grabs my attention for no particular reason, then that, too, has a high probability of being authentic.

I am sure that many of you have, at some time, received multiple signs and messages and have finally stated, "Okay, okay I got it!"

It has been said that patience is a virtue; and, in the case of wanting a sign right after a loved one has passed, it is down right true. Invite in the possibility and then let it go. Let nature take its course and let the other side decide if and when you will receive that connection you so passionately desire.

Luck of the Irish

One of the things that inspired me to write this book was an experience I had a few days after the passing of my aunt.

I had been thinking about her, all the events that preceded her passing and how it all seemed rather sudden. Family and friends returned home and things were starting to get back to a normal routine.

As I was driving down the road, thinking of other departed friends and family who had been in contact with me, I wondered if my aunt Eileen would be able to show me a sign that she was still around me and could understand my thoughts.

Wanting something to drink, I made a left turn into the parking lot of a local fast food restaurant. I then got in line in the drive-through lane and though about whether I wanted to get any food with my drink. I ordered an ice tea, and waited my turn as the cars in front of me pulled up to the drive-through window. While stopped behind the car in front of me, I glanced out my open driver-side window, and noticed the manicured landscape around the business.

The establishment had a few well-manicured small bushes next to the building along with ground-up mulch neatly covering any exposed dirt. I was astonished when I looked down and saw a single green Shamrock sticking up through the dark, moist mulch. Was this the sign that I asked for just minutes before? I looked more carefully and a wonderful feeling of love and peace came over me when I noticed that it was a four-leaf clover.

I assume that many of the readers of this story will be familiar with the rarity of finding a four-leaf clover and the significance of theist being the symbol of good luck. I was amazed and a little in shock as I stared at this symbol in this environment. There was no other ground cover in the area; and, the fact that I was just thinking of my aunt, made me realize that this was not a coincidence. Thinking that no one would believe me if I told them what happened, I wondered if I should get out of the car and pick the four-leaf clover,

I put my car into "park," opened my car door, got out and retrieved the plant. Still not believing that this was happening, I looked at it the clover closely and decided that I would place the lucky clover I had received into something to preserve this symbol. I then put the four-leaf clover in an empty package of chewing gum, so that I would have the proof to show others of the sign that I had received.

The car ahead of me pulled forward, and I continued up to the drive-through window, paid for my order and drove away. Arriving home a few minutes later, I called a friend to tell her what had just happened. She was amazed and immediately told me that it was definitely a sign. I mentioned to her that I had the four-leaf clover and that I would bring it to her home, where we could preserve it so that I would have it for the rest of my life.

The next day, I was planning to visit my friend and decided to leave the clover in its protective package that I had originally put it in.

As typically happens throughout our lives, our plans can and will change at the last minute. My expected rendezvous with my friend did not occur the next day and we did not get a chance to see each other for another three days. When we did finally get together, I opened the gum container to show her the evidence that I had obtained. To my dismay, the plant had started to dry up and was beginning to lose its shape. It still retained enough of its makeup for her to see and agree that it was an actual four-leaf clover. We agreed that preserving it even now, would not guarantee that it would retain its original look.

When talked about this special occurrence and how it brought great relief and joy to my heart, my friend told me that sharing with me the sign I had received had brought her warmth and a smile to her face. What made this particular sign so evident was not only the fact that I had just been thinking of my deceased aunt, for whom we just had a service and burial for a few days before, but the fact that she had picked that particular Irish symbol.

Both sides of my aunt's family had come from Ireland, and she was very connected to her Irish culture. Since the clover is a major symbol of Ireland, I had arranged for a floral display in the shape of the shamrock, a three-leaf clover, to be displayed next to her casket. We had also arranged for an Irish bagpiper to play throughout the service. We thought that gesture would be appropriate in that our loving aunt would have greatly appreciated the significance.

After thinking about my aunt, asking for a sign and being exposed to that specific symbol made the event a wonderful emotional experience.

A week later, I was thinking that I wished that I had not procrastinated about trying to preserve the clover from the drive-through restaurant. By now, it was shriveled up; and, we had disposed of it.

In the back of my mind, I wondered if it really had happened or, perhaps, I just wanted a sign at that time. Was it actually a rare four-leaf clover or was it some other plant, that in its infancy, could have been mistaken by me to be this contact symbol. I began to feel guilty for doubting that this event actually occurred. I wanted to ask for an additional sign, but I realized that I should be happy and satisfied that I had received even one. Next, I apologized to my deceased aunt for not preserving the sign that she had sent to me.

The following day, my friend and I decided to go to the beach. The weather had been nice, and it would be a relaxing time for us to spend out in nature. After enjoying a beautiful day, we made plans for that evening. When one is at the beach or out in nature, time has a way of flying by. We soon realized that if we wished to go out that evening we had better pack up and get back to our car.

I grabbed the cooler, she grabbed the towels and off we went through a small grove of trees towards the parking lot. Realizing how late it was caused me to walk briskly and my friend joined me, as she too realized that the day was slipping away. Continuing our *conversation in full stride as we approached the parking lot, I suddenly came to a full stop. For some reason, I looked down at the ground and there directly in front of me was a patch of clover. I immediately bent down, hearing my companion say, What are you doing?" I focused on a particular clover. I immediately picked the one to which I been drawn and we examined it more closely. My companion exclaimed, "Don't tell me!" I grinned and she then let out a scream when we both noticed it was a four-leaf clover!*

While walking at full stride in the middle of a field of trees, I had discovered what I wanted my aunt to show me again, a sign that she was still around me and happy to satisfy my request.

Immense joy and happiness now replaced my guilt and doubt as I realized that our loved ones can hear our prayers.

The second lucky four-leaf clover is now preserved under glass for all to see and understand how the process of receiving a sign can be experienced.

Joe Higgins

Part Four
Accepting & Releasing

EIGHTEEN

Letting Go and Accepting Life

❦

(Channeled from my guides)

It is very important for people to understand that their life is not about the physical and materialistic world that they think they live in. It is actually about their spiritual growth. Life's lessons have a tendency to have dual purposes; and, many times, you focus on the physical and immediate results of your actions and consequences. These results are only part of the growth of your soul, and many of you miss the opportunity to realize the true lessons that you are experiencing and how they affect the growth of your spirit.

It seems that most of you are caught up in the day-to-day activities of your life experiences and are not able to shed this daily weight that you have put around your ankle. One day leads into the next, into the next, into the next. Your accumulations produce anxiety, stress, and a whole host of detrimental effects upon your physical, emotional and spiritual body.

In order to continue to grow on a spiritual level, you must release much of this so-called baggage that you insist on carrying with you throughout your life. Many of the trials and tribulations that you encounter along your life's path resonate with you into other lessons. Learning from experience has its vast advantages in your growth potential, but it also has a downside. This downside is taking old emotional feelings from past experiences and bringing them into new life lessons you may learn in the future. In order to learn a new lesson, you must accept the situation for what it is and experience the grief and sorrow, joy and hope without relating them to past emotional experiences that may have had other situations attached to it.

The point we're trying to make is not to try to carry forward all the negative emotional and physical baggage that you've accumulated throughout your life, as this will cause you to be weighted down and to miss out on the true meaning of your lives.

Your life's true meaning is spiritual growth and enlightenment of your conscious mind to higher levels of existence. You do this by going through various tasks and learning opportunities. Throughout your life, you are given tools to deal with these events; and, it is important that you use these tools to help yourself along the way.

Many people do not realize that they have these weapons to protect themselves and to stimulate their minds and hearts along their path.

Smiling is one small technique that can enable your body to resist outside influences that might affect your growth potential. Honoring your loved ones and yourself is a high priority. This puts a natural protection around you so that when you do come into areas of influence that are not of the highest or best for you, you will have protection already in place. Sometimes, you have to deal with individuals and situations that may be difficult or draining; but, you have the natural ability to ward off these encounters and to sustain yourself in a natural state of grace.

Laughter is one of the greatest tools that you have been permitted to have on your physical life plane. For it not only protects you in difficult situations, it also has the ability to heal you on many different levels. The ability to laugh actually can promote interaction with many others, thus, it is not limited to the individual. It can change the energy in and around an individual, an event or even certain environments.

The physical ramifications of enjoying laughter can be seen in the observance of your physical body. Stress is relieved, blood pressure is lowered, anxiety dissipates and an overall feeling of wellness occurs. Joyful events can also increase the body's ability to heal itself and to bring healing to others.

Your life should not be avoided and thought of as a task; although, at times, you may feel this way. Look at the lessons that you have learned or are in the process of learning and you'll begin to see that life is a fluid process. By this we mean, it flows in and around you and you are actually an observer of the events that are occurring to your physical body. Your spiritual essence can tap in and learn from these experiences; but, at times, you have not been able to distinguish between the two. What we mean by this is people have a tendency to take things very personally when certain events occur to or around them. Your spiritual body is not as judgmental as your physical existence makes you think. Unfortunately, you all have a tendency to judge yourselves compared to others and you only set yourself up for disappointment and disapproval.

You need to realize that, as an individual spiritual entity, while you're experiencing life's lessons and learning to grow, you are actually living out your true meaning. This will not be affected by the way other individuals see or judge you.

Author's Comments:

Over the years, one of the main things that I've noticed when giving mediumistic readings is that often loved ones will come through and talk about how certain events or certain people should not take up our time, thoughts or energy when we are on the physical plane.

They even laugh about certain events that might have seemed stressful to them while they were here; because, they realize that, actually, such situations were not as significant as what had been thought. Our departed loved ones all want us to enjoy our lives, and they realize that there are difficult situations and times we must all go through; but, they don't wish us to dwell on any negative or pointless emotions.

Many times they will tell us to move on and get over it. I think that, from their perspective, they could see how much emotional stress we were able to put into certain situations but that it was just not necessary.

Our deceased who have passed on sincerely wish for us to let go, to accept life as it is and to take note of the important things –such as loving each other and loving ourselves. This is such a common message that comes through many readings that we should take heed of it and try to live our lives accordingly.

Answer from an Angel

Having been married for twenty-five years and widowed for just less than two years, I recently began dating. I had met a couple of men who, while nice enough, just did not spark any real interest. Then, I met a man who I really liked. We spoke on the phone for a while and then agreed to meet for dinner. We had a great time; and, at the end of the evening, he promised to call. I left so excited, worried that he wouldn't call, yet nervous that he would.

He did call the next day; and, although I was 46 years old, I felt like a seventeen-year-old girl all over again. I was so excited and happy. It was a warm spring day in May, and I remember the sunny sky looking a bit brighter than usual.

Later, on that same afternoon, I was in my car running errands. Beginning to get anxious about this new situation, as was the norm while driving, I spoke to my deceased husband, Jay. I asked, "Did you ever think we'd be in this position? What should I do? Is this ok? Am I ready for this? Are you ok with this?" Different emotions were swirling in my head, from happiness and excitement, to fear and guilt. I was looking for answers, and asking for help.

Pulling up to the stop light around the corner of my house, I noticed a white van stop beside me. There was a man driving; and, when he caught my eye, he motioned for me to roll down my window. Thinking he was asking for directions, I complied. Instead, he said, "I just wanted to say hello to a beautiful woman." I rolled my eyes, and made a face, thinking, "This guy is an idiot." Then, he said, "No, listen, you are fine, you are really fine. It is ok, you are fine." His tone of voice was not an, I want to pick you up tone; it was a person just saying that it is ok, you are well, everything is alright. As the light changed, he said, "Now, you have a good day, because you just made mine." Then, he drove away. I sat for what seemed like an eternity; but, in reality, it was only seconds. I drove home crying, with every hair on my body standing up. I was very glad my house was right around the corner, because I was pretty shaken up.

I knew that Jay had sent me a message, letting me know that everything was ok and that he was glad for me. He had given me his blessing to be happy. I had experienced other little signs since he passed but nothing that obvious. Sometimes, things would happen, and I would find myself second-guessing what I thought was a sign from him. However, this time there was no doubt, this was a clear sign that could not be mistaken for anything else.

When I told people what happened, everyone had the same reaction. They got "goose bumps" and every single person said the same thing before I could even finish the story: "That was a sign from Jay, letting you know it is time to move on and be happy."

Receiving that message from Jay meant the world to me. It comforted me, gave me peace, and made me feel so much better about moving on with my life, while, at the same time, letting me know he was there and that he is ok, too.

Nina M.

NINETEEN
How to Live while Waiting for a Sign
and
How to Accept Life Without Signs
❧

(Channeled from my guides)

*M*ost people understand that there is a connection between them and their loved ones, even though the loved ones have moved on through the passing of their physical bodies. These people understand the limitations of the physical lifespan, even though they are, at times, frightened by it. They do realize that it is a natural part of the living experience.

What we have seen is that, usually, right after a loved one or friend has passed over, people begin to remember them with fond memories, distinct experiences, and in social events that surrounded them. This outpouring of emotion and love is very strong on our side. We can feel the loving energy emanating from each individual towards us. We are new to our fresh surroundings; and, while trying to acclimate to this existence, we are still very much in touch with your side. At times, we are bombarded with requests for some sign to be given to let others on the physical plane know that we are safe and that we have made it to the other side.

We are able to handle multiple requests at once and we say this with smile, as at times we feel like we are taking meal orders at a drive-through window. As these requests come through, we organize them into different categories. What we mean by categories is that we try to understand and interpret the capabilities of those who are making the request. We must attempt to figure out who will be most receptive to a particular sign at a particular time. Some of the requests come from people who are not able to receive the sign for various reasons.

Some of these reasons might consist of their being too emotionally confused to be able to understand and accept a sign at this time. Others may be preoccupied with events surrounding the loved one's death and would not be able to focus on a sign, even if it were given. And still others would not be accepting of a sign, even though they may have requested one. They have not accepted the fact that they truly would be able to witness such a sign.

So, all this information, from each individual, has to be properly noted so that we may begin to work with your loved one in teaching them how to communicate through signs. The process begins when the communication from a loved one passes from one side to the other. Who will receive the signs, when and where has been agreed-upon. As we discussed earlier, sometimes a sign might come through a friend or distant relative in the hopes that they will pass that sign and message along to an immediate family member or friend who may not be able to receive the sign due to some of the reasons we listed above.

It is very important that people realize that we want to provide a sign to you. However, there are certain procedures that must be met before any sign can be attempted. Some people will receive a sign immediately or within a few days of the passing, while others may see it or connect with it in the first few months. Still others might be contacted down the line. This depends on the individual who will be receiving the sign, and how we designate their ability to handle, accept and understand the information that we provide.

We want to make it known that people should continue with the grief process. That is a naturally occurring event as one of your loved ones passes. It is especially important to some people, because grief can be an all-consuming emotional and physical state that might actually prohibit any sign or contact from coming through. It is something that must be dealt with on the physical plane, as well as through your emotional heart and through your own individual spirituality.

Each individual is different in their accepting and dealing with the process known as death. All this is taken into account, while deciding the who, when, where and how of signs of communication being achieved from one side to the other.

It is important to understand that one should not dwell on waiting for a sign, as this would not be your proper method of maintaining your life. A sign is an add-on. A connection is a bonus, a special moment between two living entities. But you must remember that you have individual lessons and learning to achieve while you are still on the physical plane. To hold back from gaining insight and learning from the process of losing a loved one is in itself a lost opportunity to learn and grow. This can take time and it should. It may be more important not to be given a sign, as your learning process may be interrupted or altered by having a sign revealed to you.

To be able to accept the passing of a loved one is the ability to continue on your life's path and is an extremely valuable lesson, for it teaches acceptance, patience, understanding and your ability to see yourself as an individual while in your physical form, separate from other entities. The love you have for a cherished one who has crossed over is still the same. That love will never change, whether you receive a sign or you don't. That is one of the magnificent things about love. It cannot be lost just because of the transition to what you call death.

So it is important to realize not to put all your hopes and aspirations into trying to connect with a passed love one, as you can become despondent when you do not hear or feel that there is any connection left between the two of you. This is just the way in your situation. It is not unusual, not special; it just is. Your wishes and hopes are still understood and accepted in the loving presence of a family member or friend who has passed and will still be around you to guide, support and participate in your life. Just because you did not receive a sign, you still need to believe that they are still around and interacting with you. Put trust in your heart and put trust in the love that you have for the deceased. This trust will sustain you throughout your continuing years, until you, too, make the transition and once again are in the presence of you loved ones.

Realize that learning some of the techniques that we are explaining in this book will open up the avenues of communications to more people and make it easier for us to determine who is able to accept and receive a sign of communication from us. It will put certain people into certain categories where they'll be able to see a sign, accept and understand the sign that perhaps they would not have been able to before.

One of our true wishes and gifts for you is to be able to help train people on your side to be more open and accepting of the signs that their loved ones are trying to communicate to them. We hope that many people will take advantage and learn from this book and be able to have the possibility of being in a receptive position, if they need to be, when a loved one from our side comes calling.

For some, life will continue as usual, and they still will not be able to see the sign, even though they have read about them or even tried to learn. To these people, it will be a tremendous loss of an opportunity to connect. But, for others, who in the past have not been able to receive a sign, perhaps with this knowledge, a few may soon be able to communicate with their loved ones. This could happen even though in the past they were unqualified to be a receiver due to various expectations and reasons.

We hope that people do not take personally the explanations and reasons for why some get signs and some don't get signs. It takes a complex amount of evaluation and understanding on our part to make the whole process work. Sometimes, we just can't find the right way to communicate with you, even though you might be wide open and accepting of anything that comes through. In that case, we have failed our part; but, perhaps, at some other time or location, we can try again.

So, never lose hope. Continue to interact with your past loved ones by talking to them, asking for advice and insight. If it is possible they will answer you through whichever method is more easily understandable. Keep your mind open to the possibilities; and, in doing this, the door of communication will open and the opportunities for contact will be born.

Author's comments:

It is important to remember that when we lose a loved one or someone we may have known, we have to experience the natural grieving process. The guides and the departed seem to understand this. We can gain great relief from knowing that our loved ones successfully have made it to the other side and that they are trying to connect to us, to inform us of their continuing existence.

We still have to deal with the missing physical being that we have been used to seeing, touching and interacting with. This is a process that will have to be dealt with by individuals in their own due time.

This process should not be held up by one who is waiting for a sign in order to move on, as the sign may not come at all. The guides stated the various reasons why this may not occur. Our progression on this physical plane depends on moving forward and dealing with every situation, both joyous and tragic. Waiting to deal with the loss of our loved ones because we have not yet received a sign would be unfortunate, unhealthy and would stagnate our growth opportunities.

The Flea Market

After my aunt had been dead for about a month, one early Sunday morning, as we often did in the past, my husband and I, decided to go to the local flea market. It was a beautiful, warm day and we thought it would be nice to get out and walk around. Right after we arrived, he drifted off to look at tools and I went to browse the aisles. As I strolled in the nice clean air I remember thinking, "Gee, Aunt Eileen, why have you not contacted my brother or me lately?"

I then thought to myself, "Oh, it is silly to wonder that. I'm sure she's just fine." Just about two minutes later, I found myself rummaging through a table of costume jewelry on which there was a tower, which had necklaces and charms hanging from it. I reached up and turned the tower once to the right; and, immediately there before me, there was a gold necklace with a charm which spelled out "Eileen." My aunt had a wonderful collection of charms she had assembled over the years, and she had been fond of buying charms for me as gifts. This was a gift from her that she didn't have to buy, but it was just as precious to me as any other charm in her collection.

Maureen R.

TWENTY

Relying on Others to Validate Yourself

❦

(Channeled from my guides)

*V*alidation is something that we see every human being trying to achieve at some point in their development. We see it as a stepping stone as to what level an individual has achieved by seeing how one's self image of himself or herself grows in the understanding that only they are capable of validating their own life.

As humans continue to learn and grow, many will look for validation from others and will base their self-awareness on these comments. People have a tendency to learn from observing different situations and interactions. It is through these observation techniques that people begin to develop ideas about how to live their lives.

Some people will be so judgmental of themselves that, at times, it will cripple their ability to grow and learn. All people have a tendency to feel better about themselves when a loved one or friend comments on something positive that they have done.

Others will look for constant feedback from everyone they come in contact with. These interactions are self-destructive, as the validation that is sought is rooted in self-doubt and low self-esteem.

Once your loved ones have passed over and can see life from a different perspective, they soon realize that the power, which they created themselves and gave up to others was unnecessary and created an obstacle to opportunities and happiness. They realize that their true spiritual essence was all that was needed to move along their pathway on the physical plane. Much time and energy was wasted on looking for and empowering others in the search for validation of who they thought they were.

Once on the other side, they could see much more clearly who they really are and how they have affected others lives, while existing on the physical plane.

It is important that the advice from our side be looked at and analyzed concerning the validation that individuals seek about their true essence. For many times, when one is on the physical plane, the rule of measurement is often askew. People have a tendency to judge themselves and others by materialistic things. Status, success, and monetary abundance are all measurements of how people feel about themselves. The real validation is not about the materialistic world; it is about tapping into your true spiritual nature.

When the money is gone, the job is finished and your health has left you wanting answers, you will begin to understand who you are. Many people go through extraordinary circumstances in their lives and have an awakening about who they truly are; and, then, they understand the true meaning of life. Those who have learned from these lessons will grow and move forward in their development. Others continue to make the same mistakes and do not take the opportunity to learn from mishaps in their lives; and, therefore, they miss the possibility of enhancing their souls.

Do not let your life be in the control of others by giving up your ability to validate yourself. Do not let others persuade you that how you are living and developing is not the way it is supposed to be. You are on the physical plane to show support and love to others and they have the responsibility to do the same to you. If someone does not wish to validate you with the proper respect and understanding that you deserve, then this is not a person you wish to associate with, as they will stunt your growth and put more obstacles in your path than are necessary.

Learn to let go of what others think about you, open your heart and let the love flow out and around you. Give it to others and you will receive it back in the pure essence of your own existence.

Author's Comments:

Often, through my mediumistic readings I've come across departed loved ones who tell their relatives and friends how proud they are of them and that they only need to look within themselves to see the true beauty that each one of us holds within our heart.

It always amazes me how our loved one's have given us a glimpse into how we should accept ourselves on our journey of growth and discovery. They teach us what is truly important in our lives and can show us this even before they pass over to the other side. Their message is to focus on our true essence of compassion and love. Forget what others think and say, live your own life, make your own mistakes and have fun along the way.

TWENTY ONE

Releasing Your Grief and Accepting the Love You Deserve

❦

(Channeled from my guides)

Author's Comments:

Here are some wise insights from my guides on very important concepts that can help you to reach your full potential. Often, we hear similar advice from friends or family, but we don't put it into practice and therefore lose an opportunity to bring peace into our lives.

As we have seen many times before, when a loved one passes over to our side, they are accepted with great joy and love. They awaken to their new existence, which they have not truly experienced in some time. For in this existence they will be surrounded by loving family, friends, and guides.

However, the love which they experience can be overwhelming; and, at other times, it can be with mixed emotions due to being separated physically from loved ones remaining on the physical plane.

But, with new insights, loss of expectations and fear are more than enough to put them in a sense of comfort few have ever experienced on your physical side. As soon as the welcoming party begins, we also observe the feelings and emotions that are caused by the physical passing.

What we see and observe from your plane is grief, loss and emotional turmoil, even though this is the natural progression of your physical state and a return to your spiritual essence. There are still the emotions that are related to not being in physical contact with a loved one.

We have seen this since the beginning of time and experience the same feelings as those left on the physical plane. For we can tap into those still living and feel their experiences. This is how we understand the grief process you all go through when you experience the loss of a family member, friend or loved one. It is at this time that we began the process of gathering our information and analyzing our ability to be able to send you a sign to let you know that we have made it to the other side and that we still exist and can be present in your lives.

At these times, we often see that many people who are open and accepting of the possibility of a sign are not able to be contacted because of the emotional and physical grief process that is occurring around the time of the death.

Releasing your grief is very important for two specific reasons. First, as we have mentioned before, the grief process can interfere with the communicating methods and this could happen on many levels. A loved one can be so distraught that no matter what method we try, a sign will not be able to be comprehended; and, therefore, contact has to be postponed or even canceled.

We wish to be very careful at this sensitive time in people's lives, as a vast amount of emotions tend to bring out different reactions in different people. Some people handle the grief process more easily than others, and some will experience a change in their daily behavior for sometime to come. We understand all of these physical, emotional and mental changes happening in and around you. We understand that you must go through this process in order to get your lives back into some structured order. For you are reminded of your own mortality, when a loved one passes. This can frighten some people and others will use it as a time of reflection on their own lives. We will work at the pace of each individual so as not to rush a possible connection or, even worse, to cause more grief and sorrow.

Once the grief begins to dissipate, to a certain extent, we can commence with the process of trying to contact you. We have been watching and waiting for the right time to send the sign you have requested. Remember, you might have requested a sign simply by talking to us or placing an intention of trying to communicate.

It is our intention to see you without any pain or suffering. That is one of the reasons why we try so desperately to connect with you. We wish to let you know that we are still in contact and that you have not lost that loving connection that you had with us on the physical plane.

It is very important for you to learn to release your grief so that you are able to receive desired communications from your loved ones. Fortunately, there is no time restraint on one's ability to release the grief in order to receive a sign.

However, one of the other reasons we wish to see you release your grief has to do with your physical and emotional well-being while you are still living out your life lessons. Chronic and sustained grief from the passing of a loved one can wreak havoc on your physical, mental, emotional and spiritual bodies. We have observed this, and it brings us great distress to see a loved one tormented and grieving for such a sustained period of time. This type of grief will curtail many future learning opportunities. It will also, cause more grief, pain and suffering. You will be creating your own turmoil; and, thus, you will have to endure the manifestations that are created as a result.

One of the best things you can do to bring love and joy into a departed one's energy is to take care of yourself, to rely on some of the tools and methods that you have available to ease your burden and stress. Spend time with friends and family, tapping into your spirituality or your religious beliefs. And, of course, a simple smile and a slight laugh will bring you closer to achieving well-being.

Once this recovery begins, you start to accept the love that you deserve into yourself and you begin to express your love to those around you. Soon, the love that you have for your dear departed will resonate back into your own life and cause joy and laughter to return to your path.

Knowing that your loved one is not truly gone and that they continue on, can bring great relief, understanding and comfort to you and to others around you. It also lets you know that the continuity of life is truly continuous and that after the physical change called death, your true spiritual essence will be reunited with all those with whom you have shared love and compassion on the physical plane.

You are definitely not alone. We hear the prayers that you speak. We hear your questions and doubts. We see the confusion and turmoil that you sometimes experience. We see how you attempt to learn and live and how you are able to understand the circumstances around your life.

It is important to realize that once you cross over to our side, the learning does not stop; it just changes in its methods and procedures. The love and joy that you have experienced in the past will continue to surround you and to radiate throughout. It is important to bring this joy and love into others' lives while you are on the physical plane, as this will magnify the experiencing of these energies.

Author's Comments:

It was shown, in an earlier chapter of this book, that through the reading I had done with Chris that realizing that your loved one is still in your life and will still be experiencing the events and challenges that you will face on your path. This will be very comforting and will help reinforce your own sense of who you are.

When you are experiencing a joyful time with friends and family, remember that your love one is also experiencing the same joy, and they are not missing out on any of your life's milestones. They will be there for the births, the graduations, the marriages, the new jobs, the tragic events, and the miraculous experiences that you will have the opportunity to learn from throughout your life.

Live, laugh, cry and dance. These are simple instructions, but very potent ones when put to use. Live without fear, laugh without hesitation, cry for relief and dance throughout your existence.

TWENTY TWO

Release Your Fears and Open Your Hearts to the Possibilities

❦

(Channeled from my guides)

*T*he mechanism for releasing your fears is so complex and important that we wish for you to take time to truly understand these concepts and to be able to use them in your daily life.

Fear can be an all-encompassing, crippling energy. It has the ability to take away learning opportunities and to alter your life's true, original path. You see, by giving in and interacting with the chaotic energy of fear you are allowing your life to be altered.

The reason that we have chosen this concept for this book is that it is one of the most powerful altering energies that an individual can create on the physical plane.

Once people begin to allow fear to control their lives, it can alter the path they have chosen. Then the individual's soul is limited in many new learning opportunities.

When you begin to fear, you begin to anticipate the various outcomes to different situations. This is actually a manifestation of your thoughts, wants and lack of understanding. When you experience uncertainty and the unknown, your physical brain will input various outcomes to a certain situation. This is how the brain begins to be taught how to react in different situations. If this continues over a long period of time, it can create chronic stress, anxiety, and the inability to accept the current circumstances in your life. Now, it will become a biological manifestation that needs to be dealt with as a physical, medical condition. It is this heavily repetitive training of the brain that causes this basic response to become chronic and, at times, overwhelming to the individual.

So, the first step we wish to introduce to you is the ability to be aware of how fear can control and create havoc in one's life. There are also many other variables that can intensify this energy, both real and imagined. But, by realizing that you, as an individual, are empowering this energy and it is detrimental to your own well being and growth, you have come to the first step in the process of releasing the control that fear can have on your life.

Once you become fully aware of the control and limitations fear puts on your life, then you are able to begin the process of releasing those fears and opening your heart to the vast possibilities of growth and happiness.

As we have mentioned earlier in this book, you possess certain tools to deal with life on the physical plane; and, one of these is the ability to smile and laugh. This particular tool is very effective in dealing with fear. For once you begin to smile and create a light-hearted energy around you, it will work as a toxic influence on the energy we call fear.

Smiling and laughter are often the keys to opening one's heart; and, once your heart begins to open, fear starts to dissipate and loses its control and potency.

By understanding the true meaning of your existence on this plane, you will have the ability to begin to put your life in a new perspective. Certain activities, emotions and questions that had created fear and control of your life will soon disappear as you realize that those manifestations are meaningless to your spiritual growth.

As spiritual beings, it is important to release this life- altering energy and to begin to live the life you were meant to experience. Happiness is not just a possibility. Rather, it is part of who you are. Further, you can see it in others with whom you come into contact throughout your life.

Think of the joy and love you received from friends and family who have passed to our side. You, too, can create this love and joy for the people you interact with daily in your lives. You have the ability to create and give happiness, love, joy and hope to other spiritual beings on your plane. This is not only a possibility. Instead, it is a responsibility to all who have chosen to live on the physical plane.

As you create the love and joy in your own life and share it with your friends, family and coworkers, you will increase the awareness of what is truly important. You will understand the loving energy that you are living in, and how it compares to the loving energy you seek or have experienced from a past loved one. You, as an individual, have the ability to create love, and to disburse it around everyone who comes into contact with you.

Once you release your fears and open your heart, the opportunities for learning and creating are unlimited. At this time, the opportunities that will present themselves to you are actually manifestations of the energy that you have created around yourself. You are the direct influence in creating the possibilities for growth and opportunities for advancement. Remember to shape your attitude and focus on the possibilities, as opposed to giving in to fear, which will stunt those possibilities and create grief and suffering in your life.

Be positive, as it will affect your entire future.

Author's comments:

It is interesting that they have focused on fear in this chapter, because it really does affect our lives on a number of levels. Fears may be seen as indecisions or slight worries over a simple choice, when, in reality, they can actually alter our lives. How many of us have worried about our jobs, relationships and achievements? Is there something we always wanted to do but were afraid to go ahead and do because of the possible consequences?

It all comes down to putting limitations on ourselves and how this can limit our growth and, eventually, our happiness. The guides teach us that by opening our hearts and understanding, it is our destiny to seek out new opportunities of learning and that we will achieve our spiritual purpose.

Replace your fear with love for yourself and others and take the next step on your journey of discovery. As my mother used to say, "Try it, you just might like it."

Part Five
Living & Learning

TWENTY THREE
Learning & Living

❦

(Channeled from my guides)

*C*ommunication is a wonderful thing. When people communicate through physical and verbal signs or other means, a transfer of energy occurs; and, in the end, it is a learning experience. That is what we see when we connect to your side and open the door of an energy transfer, enabling us to help and guide you during your learning experiences, which you call life.

On this side, we also learn by watching and interacting with you. We can tell when things are going well by observing your emotions and the state of the energy that surrounds you. We wish to help you by interceding for you; but, we are not allowed to do so at times. Only when you ask for help are we allowed to give guidance.

You see, it is not our intentions to run your life for you. We cannot do this; you must learn your lessons on your own. You must live your own life in order to achieve the goals you have set before you arrived on the physical plane. We will help you as much as possible but not if you don't ask us, for it is not our right, obligation, or responsibility to interfere in your daily lives. However, we hope that you do ask us for insight and help in dealing with your daily activities and the problems you may face along your path of life, for we gain much joy by being able to connect with you and help you understand that there is more at stake than what you see at the present moment. We can see the bigger picture from the other side, as we are not boxed in to the physical world and its limitations.

Once you leave your physical body, your consciousness and soul grow exponentially, as the limitations of your physical body are dropped. Your soul and consciousness are now limitless and able to grow and expand as much as you wish. So, once you have left your body, having these extra and increased abilities enables you to be able to see how certain things throughout your life can alter the progression of your soul.

Some times, you might feel that you are just having a terrible day. However, if you actually look at the activities around you, it's not the day that's making a terrible effect upon your life. Instead, the events currently occurring in your life and the lack of control that you might have the ability to assume have placed you in this place of judgment. You see, most of the events in your daily life are only part of the larger learning experience that encompasses your entire growth objective while on the physical plane.

Further, you should not limit yourself to any ideals of living experiences while you are learning your life's lessons. We don't mean that you should live life haphazardly and take unrealistic risks in your behavior in order to relish the physical joys of your existence. However, we do wish to see you enjoy the physical part of your existence; but, try to do it in moderation. We love the word "moderation". It doesn't let us get into trouble.

Do not limit yourself or your expectations for your life and do not let others put expectation limits on you, as well. You are here on an individual basis to learn individual lessons for yourself. Some of these lessons may seem tragic while they are happening. Others may think that they are miraculous. Put them all together and they are different chapters in your life of learning.

Once you have left the physical plane and join us on the other side, you will be able to see the actions and efforts that have made up your life. You will be shown how they have affected others whom you have come in contact with and how you have influenced other people on their life paths. Some of you will be very happy with what you see and experience, while others will wish they had put more effort into the time they had living on your plane.

Do not be despondent if you think that you have given up much of your time from learning when you could have been making great strides in your development. There is always time. Understand that your true nature is to learn and to love; and, by experiencing these, you will create opportunities to share this love and learning with others on your plane. So you see, one little act or action can create a whole host of variables that will interact on both your side and on ours.

Rejoice in your living and learning experiences, as few will have the opportunity to indulge in them as you have. Yes, this is true. Many people think that everyone - every entity, every being - has the opportunity to fulfill a life's lesson on your plane. This is not entirely true, as some would not take the chance of coming to a physical plane in order to learn. They would rather sit back and observe and try to learn from that state of consciousness.

It has happened that some have not actually experienced the physical plane as you have, and the lack of understanding that they have of it creates turmoil in some other's lives because of it. These others have not matured to the level that would be necessary to accept responsibility for living on your plane. Yet, they wish to intercede, control and dabble in the daily lives of the conscious souls who are living in the physical plane. However they do have access to the dimensional level of your existence.

We do not wish to scare or interfere with people's lessons by telling them of some of the other entities that exist. We only wish to tell you that you, as an individual, have a responsibility to yourself to grow and learn. You have the ultimate control over your life. Do not see it as a day-to-day activity of working, shopping and daily responsibilities with children or taking care of elders. These are only pieces of the puzzle; and, once you pass to the other side, you will see the pieces come together in the portrait of your life, which will begin to appear to you in all of its glory and wisdom.

We have a great regard and appreciation for what each and every one of you do. Many of you have no idea of the actual input you have on others' lives - some for the good, some for so-called bad - but, eventually, you will come to understand your actions and interactions as they create a reverberating wave of energy throughout different planes of existence.

So start every day with a fresh idea that you want to help yourself understand and learn the lessons that will be in front of you that day and do it with an open heart by showing kindness to strangers. Let the love of your energy shine forth. It will bring you great joy and satisfaction even if today you are having what you think is a miserable time. Some day, you will see that precious day was actually a jewel of time. You should accept it for what it was, and create light of darkness, joy out of sorrow and understanding out of bewilderment. This is the power that you have; you are all incredibly thoughtful creatures. It is just that, at times, you do not understand the full nature of your existence.

You are part of a global, spiritual consciousness. You are in direct contact with all of the spiritual beings on your plane. You have the ability to communicate at will with each other. You can cause great joy or great suffering. You and only you have the control and the method for which direction you choose.

We understand that the decisions you make sometimes put you under great stress and sorrow. That is why we are here to help you, to hold your hand, to give you guidance. For we can see the final outlook of things to come.

We wish to hold your hands while you are experiencing some of the most stressful times of your lives. You must remember that you are never alone. We wish for you to know that we are always here for you and that you were never meant to be alone. You may feel isolated in your existence, but don't ever – not even once - think you're alone. We are always around. We are always looking after you. We are always trying to protect you.

We cannot intervene in every situation so that you do not hurt yourself or become ill. Nor can we always intervene when something tragic happens to a love one. For these may be lessons in your life that have learning opportunities associated with them. From your perspective, it is difficult to see this when it happens. It is extremely difficult when certain tragic situations happen to children, as well as to the elderly or to kind strangers.

We do not wish for you to struggle and live painful existences. Your spiritual makeup and being has much strength and operates on a high level. You will be rewarded with great love and happiness once you start to understand that the lessons that you are learning now help to deepen your understanding of the existence of life.

We understand that much of this information may seem complex, contradictory or quite frightening. By giving you this information, it is not our intention to put you in that state. We are only letting you know that there is a larger picture to your individual lives and that you are all truly connected. This is important; because, when you realize this, you will start to treat each other as special and individual spiritual beings, who are all here to learn individual, specific lessons. You are honoring each other and honoring yourself is the highest form of understanding.

We could go to great depths of awareness about this, but we will not go into it right now. However, remember and understand that by loving yourself and loving others, you have already created the divine energy around you to propel you to the highest level of education that you can achieve.

Author's comments:

It is a wonderful opportunity to be able to view the insights the guides have given us, while we are still here on this physical plane. Often, we would not be able to understand this guidance until we passed over.

These comments and this guidance give us the opportunity to enhance our knowledge of ourselves, to bring greater satisfaction to our journey and to learn to live the way we were meant to be. Any opportunity to increase our awareness of bringing more love and understanding into our lives is something that we all should take advantage of.

TWENTY FOUR
Some Day You Will Join the Party

❦

(Channeled from my guides)

On the physical plane, it is a natural factor that your lives, as you know them, will cease at a given time in your physical existence. You die. Your physiological body ends its natural cycle, and you are released from the burdens of being confined on the physical plane.

Once you are released, and you have begun your journey back to where you have come from, you are welcomed by your loved ones and guides.

We understand that many people have different cultural and religious beliefs concerning the transition referred to as death. However, we see it as an emotional and spiritual change. We do not want to offend any individual by being more specific as to the right or wrong methods of crossing and being accepted on our side.

Once you have arrived and you are greeted, you begin to realize that your true essence has always been of the spiritual realm. You realize the learning opportunities that you have engaged in and how they have affected the growth of your soul.

You now understand the methods that were used in this learning and how your loved ones who remain on the physical plane are accepting your passing.

The process begins by analyzing the possibility and opportunities of sending a sign to those on the other side. As we mentioned earlier in the book, there will not always be a sign sent for various reasons; but, it is at this point that the opportunity is fully looked at and a judgment is made as to whether to move forward or not. All the factors that we have talked about are weighed evenly to see if contact should be attempted now or, perhaps, at a later time.

The perspective that one can see, once they have passed through to our side is like one's opening their eyes for the first time after being without sight for many years. You become fully aware of everything that you have been taught and how it has affected not only you but others with whom you have come in contact. Your interactions on the physical plane are relived so that you may understand from your new perspective the events that occurred. Pain and suffering, as you are aware of on your physical plane are replaced by analysis and pondering of the results of these lessons.

You will learn how the interactions you have had with others have affected their emotional and physical well being. You will be able to see and feel how those others have interpreted your interaction with them. At times of this reflection, some people become anxious, as they realize the hurt and pain they have inflicted on others. This is when they wish they could relive certain events and deeds that they participated in when they were on the physical plane. They realize that some of the sorrow that they brought to others can only be relieved with the realization that they have misled themselves by their actions.

This is taken into account if someone needs to contact a person on the physical plane in order to apologize or to let them know that they now realize that their actions had hurt or made others feel unworthy. This is one for whom we would help make that connection in order for them to gain new ground in their development from our side.

These new arrivals have the means to correct some of the misfortune that they have brought upon themselves once they work with others on our side to help relieve suffering and misery still existing on the physical plane. There is always opportunity to move forward in one's development, even if one has neglected the opportunity to do it on the physical plane. It is unfortunate when someone does not take the opportunity to learn to grow when they are on the physical plane. Then, it has to be accomplished when they return home to the side of spirits.

An example of this might be like someone having to go to summer school after not having achieved an acceptable grade during the regular school year. Some will have to repeat one course and some others repeat many years.

Many spirits arrive on our side with joy in their hearts and peace in their souls and wish to let their loved ones, who were left on the physical plane, know that they still exist and have made it to the other side. It is a joyous time when newly arrived spirits get to mingle and coexist with all the family and friends with whom they have shared the physical plane.

Old friends who have **left the physical plane before you** and those who have **not made the journey to the physical plane** are once again reunited with you and you finally come to realize that you are surrounded with so many beautiful and loving entities.

The day you pass to our side is actually your true birthday, as you return home to a party that is indescribable in its extent.

Learn the lessons and insights that we have shown you in this book and be the loving and compassionate spiritual beings that you are capable of being. Some day we will see you at your party and the love and joy that you have given to others on the physical plane will surround you for the rest of eternity.

Contact Information

❦

If you have a story that you want to be considered for the next upcoming book please visit our Web site to submit it or you can write to:

Joe Higgins

PO Box 9212

Fall River, Ma 02720

Visit our Website for:

- Book and Audio ordering information

- Join our Mailing list for upcoming books and seminars.

Web Address

www.josephmhiggins.com

7283289R0

Made in the USA
Lexington, KY
07 November 2010